Boxing

by Wallace Matthews
International Boxing Hall of Famer

for dummies®
A Wiley Brand

Boxing For Dummies®

Published by: **John Wiley & Sons, Inc.,** 111 River Street, Hoboken, NJ 07030-5774, www.wiley.com

For general information on our other products and services, please contact our Customer Care Department within the U.S. at 877-762-2974, outside the U.S. at 317-572-3993, or fax 317-572-4002. For technical support, please visit https://hub.wiley.com/community/support/dummies.

Wiley publishes in a variety of print and electronic formats and by print-on-demand. Some material included with standard print versions of this book may not be included in e-books or in print-on-demand. If this book refers to media such as a CD or DVD that is not included in the version you purchased, you may download this material at http://booksupport.wiley.com. For more information about Wiley products, visit www.wiley.com.

Library of Congress Control Number is available from the publisher.

ISBN 978-1-394-40798-9 (pbk); ISBN 978-1-394-40800-9 (ebk); ISBN 978-1-394-40799-6 (ebk)
SKY10165585_081426

Contents at a Glance

Table of Contents

Introduction

Welcome to *Boxing For Dummies*, a book that will introduce you to what is probably humankind's oldest form of sport and one that I believe presents the greatest combination of physical conditioning, mental discipline, and mastery of complex techniques. Unlike any other sport, combat or otherwise, in boxing there are no timeouts, no tapouts, no substitutions. Once the bell rings, you have bought the ticket and you are taking the ride. And what a ride it is!

Boxing has long been called the art of self-defense, but it is really the art of self-control, the control of both the body and the mind. By the time you get done reading this book, I believe you will achieve both.

About This Book

Like a good boxing match, this book will feature a little of this and a little of that. You will learn some of the history of this ancient and noble art, from its beginnings through what is considered its golden age, and on into the future of boxing.

It is also an instruction manual geared to several audiences: those who have some experience in boxing but want to take their game to the next level, those who have always been fascinated by the intricacies of professional boxing and would like to know exactly how it's done, and those who are simply looking for a fun and effective new way to work out.

I'll also catch you up on the best ways to watch, score, and understand a boxing match, and the best outlets with which to keep up with the latest developments. You'll learn the rules of the game, the criteria by which fights are judged, where to find the best examples of great boxing and boxers, and even the best boxing writers to read, both past and present.

I can't promise this book will make you a world champion boxer or a Hall of Fame boxing writer, but it will make you a better fighter and a more discerning observer. So let's get ready to rumble!

Why Am I the One Writing This?

I am a self-confessed lifelong boxing nerd.

I spent 37 years of my first career writing and analyzing boxing matches for publications such as *New York Newsday, New York Post, New York Daily News, The New York Times,* and ESPN.com and for broadcast outlets such as NBC, CBS, HBO, and Showtime. I was lucky enough to have been ringside for what I consider one of the greatest eras of professional boxing and was privileged to cover the likes of Larry Holmes, Evander Holyfield, Marvelous Marvin Hagler, Sugar Ray Leonard, Thomas Hearns, Roberto Duran, Mike Tyson, Oscar de la Hoya, and Floyd Mayweather Jr.

Before that, I had been an amateur boxer who competed in the New York Daily News Golden Gloves and numerous amateur tournaments throughout the New York metropolitan area. Currently, I work as a personal fitness trainer and boxing coach at a YMCA on Long Island, where I am honored to share my knowledge of and enthusiasm for the sport with a wide variety of clients ranging in age from teenagers to octogenarians.

This book is a labor of love that encompasses more than a half-century of deep immersion in a sport that I consider the greatest test of a human being's courage, will, and determination.

TIP

I realize the vast majority of the readers of this book will never actually step into a ring to spar or fight. This is also true of my boxing clients, yet I train them as if they will, and I wrote this book the same way. Hey, you never know!

Foolish Assumptions

My basic assumptions are as follows:

- That you know next to nothing about boxing and wouldn't know a left hook from a fish hook
- That you are possibly a fitness enthusiast who has grown tired of CrossFit, Tabata, Pilates, and HIIT and are seeking a new way to torture your body into fighting trim
- That you are possibly an aspiring champion looking to upgrade your skills to professional level
- That you are possibly already a professional boxer who just wants to see whether I really knew what I was writing about for nearly 40 years

Icons Used in This Book

Boxing For Dummies uses icons to highlight important points for you. Keep an eye out for the following:

TIP

These helpful hints will enable you to get more out of your boxing workout or viewing experience.

REMEMBER

Just in case I feel the need to repeat myself. In boxing, repetition is everything.

FIGHTING WORDS

Master this lingo and you can navigate any boxing gym in the world.

HISTORICAL TIDBIT

Bite-sized nuggets of boxing lore to illustrate a point.

Beyond the Book

In addition to what you're reading right now, this product comes with a free access-anywhere Cheat Sheet that provides information on how to start a boxing training regimen and how to become a more knowledgeable boxing fan, among other things. To get this Cheat Sheet, simply go to `www.dummies.com` and type *Boxing For Dummies Cheat Sheet* in the Search box.

Where to Go from Here

Entirely up to you. This book can be read cover to cover, from the first punches thrown by cavemen to Oleksandr Usyk's next title defense. Or, if history is not your thing but gym time is, you can skip ahead to the workout sections and come back to read about John L. Sullivan and Sugar Ray Robinson while you're soaking in a post-workout hot tub. But make sure not to skip the sections on proper equipment and safety measures. Boxing workouts are challenging and fun, but actual boxing can be extremely dangerous. As the referee says before every fight, protect yourself at all times!

1

Your New Favorite Workout

IN THIS PART . . .

Find out why boxing will become your new favorite workout, despite its complexity and intensity. Or maybe because of it!

Read some remarkable stories about how boxing training has helped people of all ages, some with infirmities that you might think would keep them out of the gym.

Discover some of the rich history of this ancient and fascinating sport, from its origins in the bareknuckle era, through its golden age of the '20s, '30s, and '40s, to the mega-fights of today.

Learn how a boxing workout can transform your body and mind.

IN THIS CHAPTER

- » What boxing can do for your body and mind
- » Who can benefit from boxing training?
- » Am I too old? Too deconditioned? Too anything to train like a boxer?

Chapter 1
Why Boxing? Why Not!

Boxing may not be for everyone, but boxing training certainly is!

Even if you never make that four-step climb into an actual boxing ring, the skills and training methods employed by professional fighters can benefit everyone, regardless of age, gender, previous experience, or current physical condition. A well-designed boxing program will get you into great physical shape; improve your strength, stamina, reflexes, and balance; and teach you some impressive new skills.

A comprehensive boxing training program incorporates elements of High Intensity Interval Training (HIIT), strength training, cardio training, and flexibility. And it does this in a way that keeps students coming back because of the virtually endless variety of combinations that can be thrown once someone masters a mere six basic punches.

What Can Boxing Do for You?

Well, a lot of things. For one, it will strengthen your shoulders, tone and stabilize your core, and improve your cardio fitness, your balance, and your understanding of how the kinetic chain of the body — the legs, hips, core, shoulders, arms, and fists — works in coordination to produce power you didn't know you had.

It will also increase your self-confidence in both your physical abilities and your analytical and problem-solving skills, because even at the workout level, boxing provides a never-ending stream of challenges to both the mind and the body.

Is it easy? No. In fact, just about all my clients have had the same or similar reaction after their first boxing workout: "I had no idea how difficult this was!"

They were referring not so much to the physical demands of the sport but to the mental demands. And quite candidly, there are a lot of things to remember: Keep your hands up. Keep your chin down. Stay profiled to your target. Keep the correct spacing between your feet. Be mindful of your distance from your opponent. Remember to shift your weight with each punch. Reset yourself into your starting position. And so on.

You get the idea. But believe it or not, with repetition these things will eventually become second nature, as they must be for a boxer in the midst of a tough battle. Don't be discouraged by how complex it seems in the beginning. Just like learning any other discipline, such as playing a musical instrument, you must practice your patterns slowly until they become familiar, and then gradually increase your tempo until you get up to speed.

With a little dedication, it *will* happen!

The Art of Self-Control

Boxing has been called the art of self-defense, but in truth, it is the art of self-control.

That means control of both the mind and body. Boxers need to be strong, lean, agile, and both aerobically and anaerobically fit. They also need to be able to control their emotions and impulses in order to effectively execute the necessary movements of a good boxer.

Boxing training targets both these goals through a systematic approach combining physical conditioning, technical expertise, and mental discipline. Just as a world-class boxer cannot be flabby or deconditioned, neither can they be prone to anger, panic, or discouragement. The well-trained fighter is in great shape not only physically but also mentally, prepared to evaluate any situation put in front of them and ready to react appropriately.

REMEMBER

Unless you're planning to make a career of the prize ring, you will not get hurt in boxing training. You will definitely get sore, especially in the shoulders, torso, and, if you're punching correctly, in your hamstrings and calves. You might also skin your knuckles on the inside of your gloves. But all this will pass after the first couple of workouts.

In addition to the physical benefits, boxing is problem-solving. The problem, of course, is your opponent, and it's your job to figure out how to solve that person. That requires a cool head and an analytical approach to your task, no matter how chaotic things become in the ring. You'll find that this approach, when mastered, will serve you well in all aspects of your life, not just in the ring. Remember, be analytical, not reactive.

Boxing has come a long way since its origins many centuries ago. There is evidence that people were engaging in some form of hand-to-hand combat since prehistoric times. Through the centuries, boxing has evolved from the days of bareknuckle fights-to-the-finish, through the adoption of padded gloves, three-minute rounds, 15-round, and now 12-round championship fights.

But the essence of boxing has not changed. It is a form of unarmed combat requiring the skillful coordination of hands, feet, and head, and is arguably the sternest test of a human being's courage, determination, and discipline in the realm of sports.

This book aims to unravel the mysteries of what makes boxing both so great and so difficult, and to decode those mysteries so that even the rawest beginner can master them. The object is not to create fighters, but to create lean, mean fighting machines whose pugilistic pursuits are confined to the safety of the gym.

To paraphrase the words of famed ring announcer Michael Buffer, "Are you ready to rumble?"

If so, let's climb those four steps into a new world of fun and fitness.

Boxing Training Is for Everyone

John Hahn is 69 years old and for the past 10 years has suffered from Parkinson's disease. (See Figure 1-1.)

FIGURE 1-1: John Hahn says boxing training has slowed the progression of his Parkinson's disease.

with permission of Anthony Policano

Dan Schoeffler is 67 years old and three years removed from a massive heart attack. (See Figure 1-2.)

FIGURE 1-2: Dan Schoeffler had a near-fatal heart attack a year before beginning boxing training.

with permission of Anthony Policano

Mike Sanchez is 56 years old, a former NYPD officer who was blinded in the line of duty. (See Figure 1-3.)

FIGURE 1-3: Mike Sanchez, a former NYPD officer blinded in the line of duty, banging the hand pads.

with permission of Anthony Policano

What do these people have in common? All are regular attendees of a boxing class, and each has benefited greatly, both physically and mentally, from the workout.

And they are only a small sample of the incredible cross section of people who are regular attendees of my boxing classes at a fitness center on Long Island. Among my members are school teachers, lawyers, retirees, and high school students. Approximately half my members are women. I have young people with aspirations of becoming professional boxers and older people who simply want to try a new form of physical conditioning.

All have discovered that not only are they benefiting from regular boxing workouts, but that they enjoy them more than any other form of exercise they've tried.

There is Christine Lewis, 35 and pregnant with her first child, who comes to boxing class after work and intends to keep coming right up to her due date. (See Figure 1-4.) There is Erin Nostro, a 57-year-old teacher's assistant who came in knowing nothing about boxing but now is capable of throwing 160 hard, technically sound punches in the final 30 seconds of a three-minute round.

FIGURE 1-4: Christine, training through early pregnancy, intends to keep boxing right up to her due date.

with permission of Anthony Policano

There is Yvette Motta, a 55-year-old nurse at a cancer hospital and a mother of three who discovered just a couple of years ago that she is a Type 1 adult-onset diabetic. Yvette found her first boxing workout so demanding she thought she would need an oxygen tank to recover. But a few months later, she found she could get through 12 three-minute rounds of bag punching and regularly throws 150 punches in the 2-4-6-8-10 drill that comes in the final 30 seconds. (See Figure 1-5.)

"My legs are definitely stronger and my posture is better," Yvette says. "I feel like it's a complete total body workout. And it's fun."

Erin started boxing after experiencing a life-threatening heart issue a couple of years ago. "It was a little intimidating at first," she admits. "But I was looking for something different and nothing else was getting my heart rate up to where I wanted it. This gets me really out of breath and my core strength has really improved. I love it!"

When class is not in session, Erin often comes in on her own after work just to hit the bags. (See Figure 1-6.)

Which brings me to Gerry McGrath, 71 years old, 6-foot-3, and 300 pounds, who, despite undergoing cancer surgery a few months after taking up boxing, has become a devotee to the point where he installed a heavy bag in his garage for impromptu workouts between classes. And trust me when I tell you he has learned how to transfer every ounce of those 300 pounds into his right cross. (See Figure 1-7.)

FIGURE 1-5: Yvette's boxing workouts are helping her manage her Type 1 diabetes.

with permission of Anthony Policano

FIGURE 1-6: Don't let Erin's smile fool you. She is a dynamo on the bags and mitts.

with permission of Anthony Policano

FIGURE 1-7: Gerry is a big man with a big punch.

with permission of Anthony Policano

"Taking boxing has brought out my competitiveness again, after years of inactivity," he says. "My cardio has definitely improved. At first I couldn't get through three minutes but now I can, easily. I just feel better overall, and it gives me something to look forward to."

Doctors have known for years that a boxing workout can greatly benefit patients suffering from Parkinson's, the disease that robbed Muhammad Ali of his incredible grace and athleticism for the last three decades of his life. The international program known as Rock Steady Boxing has been clinically proven to slow the decline of Parkinson's. John Hahn, who has battled Parkinson's for 10 years, finds that the combination of movement and coordination required for a boxing workout has helped to slow the progression of the disease.

"To sit in front of the TV and drink a beer and rot away was not my plan," Hahn says. "Boxing definitely helps me."

To augment his workouts, I will occasionally shout out a math problem to John while he's hitting the pads or ask him to name a state capital. Combining a cognitive test along with the physical workout is immensely beneficial to Parkinson's sufferers.

Dan, who has an engineering degree from Princeton, is tall and lean and athletic. And he was all those things back in 2023 when in the midst of a dumbbell workout he suddenly experienced a tightness across his chest. He went to the hospital and came out five days later with six stents. Turns out he had had a heart attack caused by a 95 percent blockage in an artery.

"I was this close to sending out funeral invitations," he said.

Instead, he joined a boxing class at his local YMCA. "I liked it immediately," he said. "It improved my stamina, my balance, my upper body strength, and my confidence. And it's helped me learn new things. I could never jump rope before, but now I can."

Despite his litany of infirmities brought on from years of athletics, Mike Prestia says that boxing class actually provides a respite from the pain.

"It takes everything inside, all the anger that's built up from all these aches and pains and it's like a release," he says. "I actually feel good when I come here. I feel like I've gotten stronger and after the workout, I feel light and airy, like a feather. It takes the lead out."

A true profile in courage and determination is the story of Alex MacPherson, who, despite missing his left hand due to a birth defect, has taught himself to golf and bench press and recently took up boxing as a way to stay fit and bond with his two sons. (See Figure 1-8.)

"The best thing my parents ever did was push me out the front door and say, 'Go do what everyone else is doing,'" he says.

Alex played high school football and even led his team in interceptions one year. In the boxing gym, he wraps his left arm to keep the glove from sliding off, and punches away with both hands. You would never know he was any different from any of the other boxers in the class.

"I don't set limitations for myself," he says. "I just find a way to go and do it."

But the most remarkable story, and beneficiary, of a boxing workout has got to be Mike Sanchez, who was blinded in a job-related incident while an NYPD officer more than 20 years ago.

"I like doing things that other blind people have not done," he says. "What I like about boxing is that it's different from the other exercise classes. It's all about rhythm and timing. I'm in rhythm with my punching bag. I'm visualizing the bag moving and then coming towards me and I time my punches accordingly." (See Figure 1-9.)

Of course, you don't need to be recovering from a major illness or injury to be attracted to or benefit from a boxing workout.

FIGURE 1-8: Despite being born without a left hand, Alex goes through a vigorous boxing workout.

with permission of Anthony Policano

FIGURE 1-9: Mike Sanchez hitting the heavy bag.

with permission of Anthony Policano

Walter Bast, 44, is a neuroscientist with a PhD in physics who has the lean body of a gymnast. He began boxing as a workout in his native Argentina in his 20s and has continued steady boxing training after emigrating to New York. (See Figure 1-10.)

"It's been great for my body. I'm in much better shape than I used to be," he says. "But the best thing I got from my boxing training is more confidence."

FIGURE 1-10: Walter is a neuroscientist who took up boxing in his native Argentina.

with permission of Anthony Policano

Andrea Calabretta is 62, a former hairdresser who recently reentered the workforce as an office manager and describes herself as "semi-athletic." She ventured into the boxing class because "it looked cool and it looked challenging."

She wasn't sure if she was coordinated or strong enough to keep up with the routine, but after her first class, she found out she was. Now, Andrea says, "I was addicted. I loved it right away."

"I knew nothing when I started. I grew up with all sisters. We fought in different ways," she says. "But the repetition of it taught me how to box and how to punch and it forces you to challenge yourself. Each class you feel a little stronger and you feel more confident in the way you're punching." (See Figure 1-11.)

The effect has been apparent in her home as well. "My boyfriend noticed my arms are getting bigger," she says. "He was like, 'What are you doing with those arms?'"

Mari D'Alessandro, 75, is an avid tennis player whose dedication to learning technique and mastering the transfer of weight from her legs through her hips and finally to her shoulders has shown benefits on the tennis court. (See Figure 1-12.)

"I hit my forehand like a rocket now," she says.

FIGURE 1-11: Andrea working on the heavy bag.

with permission of Anthony Policano

FIGURE 1-12: Mari says her boxing training has made her a terror on the tennis court.

with permission of Anthony Policano

Kevin Cooper, a former vice president of operations for Minute Man Press, had something of a background in combat sports, having taken several years of kick-boxing in his 60s. But the COVID era sent him to the sidelines until 2024, when at the urging of his wife, Rose Ann, a regular participant in a boxing class, he decided to give boxing a try.

Almost immediately, he saw physical effects. Aside from the cardio benefits, Kevin noticed something else. "I can really feel it in my arms and my shoulders," he says. When I put my shirts on, there's a difference now. Even more so than from kickboxing."

And there's a psychological benefit as well: "When you land a good punch and hear that crack on the pad, it makes you excited. Wow!" (See Figure 1-13.)

FIGURE 1-13: Kevin, a big puncher, gets motivated by the crack of his gloves against the mitts.

with permission of Anthony Policano

Boxing Training Costs Little but Returns Much

Unlike many other training programs, the monetary investment in a boxing program is minimal. A decent pair of gloves can be found for under $50, and a set of hand wraps can be had for less than $10. (A full explanation of boxing equipment with representative prices is covered in Chapters 5, 6, and 7.) There's no need for expensive shoes or workout gear; standard athletic shoes, shorts, and a T-shirt are sufficient to get you started. And if you join a properly equipped gym, the rest of the modalities you will need — heavy bags, speed bags, jump ropes — will be provided for you. (See Figure 1-14.)

FIGURE 1-14: Yvette and Andrea going through a hand pad drill.

with permission of Anthony Policano

The real investment you must make in boxing training is your time and dedication. Almost every client I've trained has had the same initial reaction ("I had no idea how much went into this!") because in all candor, boxing done correctly requires a great amount of precision, which takes some dedication to learn. But I have found through practical experience that once you get a taste of what it feels like to throw and land a good punch against a bag or a pair of mitts and hear that satisfying *crack!*, you'll enjoy the same sensation enjoyed by my students.

"I really like the feeling of the impact of the punches," says Andrea.

Or, in the words of Kevin, "Wow!"

IN THIS CHAPTER

- How it all began
- Adopting the Marquis of Queensbury Rules
- Boxing's Golden Age (1919–1964)
- On to the present-day

Chapter 2

From Bare Knuckles to Oleksandr Usyk: Tracing the History of Modern Boxing

Before human beings had weapons, they had fists, and the type of unarmed combat that evolved into boxing as we know it today has existed in some form since the dawn of humankind. Historians trace rudimentary forms of boxing back to ancient Egypt and Ethiopia, where it is believed it originated, and it eventually spread to ancient Greece and Rome.

But boxing as we know it did not appear in Europe — England, to be precise — until the late 16th century, when fights were contested with bare knuckles, essentially governed by no formal rules and without round lengths or time limits. As a result, fights were virtually an "anything goes" affair, and contestants were free not only to punch opponents but to kick them, head-butt them, and gouge their eyes. Rounds generally ended when one fighter was knocked — or often, thrown or wrestled — to the ground. This did not necessarily stop the downed fighter from being kicked or stomped by his upright opponent.

Beginnings: The Bareknuckle Era

The first recorded British boxing champion was James Figg, a man of great foresight who not only fought but also promoted boxing matches, realizing that money could be made through the selling of tickets to watch two other men fight. Figg is said to have fought 271 bouts without a defeat. But a greater impact on the sport was wrought by Jack Broughton, who introduced the "Broughton Rules," which prohibited continuing to strike a fighter who was on the ground, and established the use of a 30-second count over a downed fighter. If the fighter could not rise within the 30 seconds, he was declared a loser. Broughton also introduced a form of padding to be worn over the fists during sparring, although not in an actual fight. Broughton was prompted to create these rules after inflicting a fatal beating upon challenger George Stevenson in 1741, the first recorded death in a boxing ring. The Broughton Rules were the forerunner of the Marquis of Queensbury Rules, which were introduced in 1867 and continue to be used, with some modifications, to this day.

Other notable fighters of the era were Daniel Mendoza, recognized as the first Jewish boxing champion; Jem Mace, one of the first boxers to be recognized as a World Heavyweight Champion; Samuel Elias, who fought under the name Dutch Sam and was considered the hardest hitter of his era, which spanned 1801–1814; and Tom Hickman, a light-heavyweight known by the colorful nickname "The Terrible Gas Man," a soubriquet that had nothing to do with digestive troubles but was a reference to his day job.

The Marquis of Queensbury Era

Although they were named for a British nobleman of the Victorian era, the Marquis of Queensberry Rules were actually written in 1865 by John Graham Chambers, a Welsh sportsman with an interest in boxing. The Queensbury Rules, officially adopted in 1867, required the use of boxing gloves during matches and established the three-minute round, the one-minute rest period, and the 10-second count for a knockout, all of which continue to be used today. But the lengths of championship bouts could vary according to the laws of a particular jurisdiction.

The first heavyweight championship match to be fought with gloves occurred on September 7, 1892, between John L. Sullivan, a pure slugger known as the Boston Strong Boy and the first American to be recognized as a World Heavyweight Champion (see Figure 2-1), and James J. (Gentleman Jim) Corbett, who embodied a new style featuring footwork, defense, and slick boxing. The fighters wore five-ounce gloves, barely larger than driving gloves and half the size of the gloves worn by heavyweights today. Corbett, 24, wore down the 34-year-old Sullivan and knocked him out in the 21st round to become the first heavyweight champion of the gloved era.

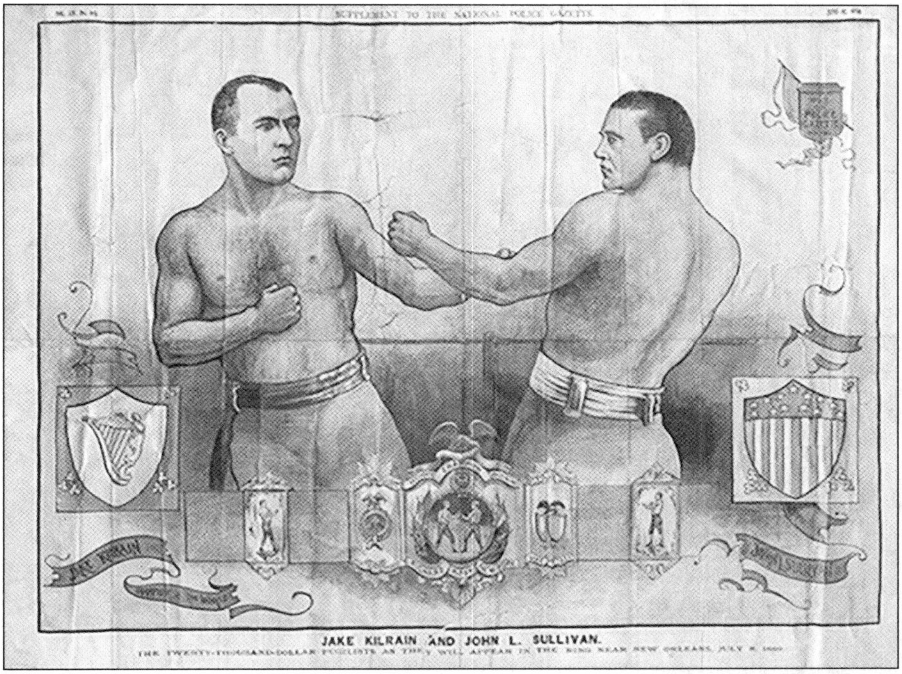

FIGURE 2-1: The bareknuckle bout between John L. Sullivan and Jake Kilrain went 75 rounds and lasted more than two hours.

National Police Gazette / Wikimedia Commons / Public domain

Jack Johnson and the First Great White Hope

Jack Johnson, of Galveston, Texas, became the first Black heavyweight champion of the world by knocking out Australian Tommy Burns in 14 rounds on December 26, 1908. (See Figure 2-2.) Johnson was a flamboyant figure who enraged White America with his refusal to be subservient. He flaunted his interracial romances, taunted his opponents, and frequently flashed his bankroll and his mouthful of gold teeth. In an era of blatant racism, this caused many to seek a White challenger to dethrone Johnson. At the time, like major league baseball, boxing operated under a "color line," and Black boxers essentially fought in a separate league and competed for segregated titles. Some of the era's notable Black heavyweights who never got a shot at the "world" title were Sam McVea, Joe Jeannette, Harry Wills, and Sam Langford, whom Jack Dempsey admitted was the only man he ever feared.

Johnson held the World Colored Heavyweight Championship for four years before defeating Burns, and never fought a Black challenger as the World Heavyweight Championship, believing the public would not pay to see two Black men fight for the title. Hence the hunt for what became known as "The Great White Hope."

FIGURE 2-2: Jack Johnson defeats Tommy Burns to become the first Black heavyweight champion.

Unknown author / Wikimedia Commons / Public domain

Former heavyweight champion James J. Jeffries, who had not fought in six years, was recruited for the task, but was brutally knocked out in the 15th round of a one-sided bout in Reno, Nevada, on July 4, 1910. The result so enraged the crowd that police had to be brought into the ring to protect Johnson and maintain order, and the ensuing race riots around the country ensured that boxing's color line would be kept in place indefinitely. As a result, only two Black fighters were given a shot at the heavyweight title over the next two decades before Joe Louis became the second Black heavyweight titleholder in 1937.

After the Jeffries bout, Johnson was forced into virtual exile, pursued by law enforcement for allegedly violating the Mann Act, which prohibited transporting women across state lines for "immoral purposes," an obscure law selectively enforced upon Johnson because he was married to a White woman. In 1912, he emigrated to Paris and made his last three title defenses outside the United States. Johnson lost his title by knockout to Jess Willard in Havana, Cuba, in 1915. Johnson later claimed to have thrown the bout, but this claim is generally believed to have been fabricated by a financially strapped Johnson to sell a magazine story later in life.

In many ways, Johnson was the Jackie Robinson of boxing, although his fighting style and personal style more resembled that of Muhammad Ali, who would succeed Johnson as heavyweight champion a half-century later. And the defeat of Johnson by Willard paved the way for the Golden Age of boxing and the rise of professional sports' first real superstar.

The Modern Era (1919–Present)

Jack Johnson's successor, Jess Willard, failed to ignite much of a reaction, positive or negative, in the boxing public. Although he stood 6-6 and weighed in the neighborhood of 250 pounds, Willard was a soft-spoken and not particularly aggressive man who admittedly did not enjoy boxing and pursued it only for the money that financed his farm in Kansas. He defended his title just once in four years before being persuaded to take on a rising young heavyweight out of Manassa, Colorado, who had run up an impressive string of knockouts. The young heavyweight's name was Jack Dempsey. (See Figure 2-3.)

FIGURE 2-3: Jack Dempsey, boxing's first superstar, in 1926.

Wide World Photos / Wikimedia Commons / Public domain

Dempsey was a rough-hewn character who had left home at 12, ridden the rails as a hobo, and lived a hand-to-mouth existence bankrolled mainly by fighting older men in bars as a teenager, after which he would pass around a hat for donations. When he hooked up with Jack (Doc) Kearns, a slick boxing manager with a shrewd sense of public relations, his professional career took off. Dempsey did not fight like most of the heavyweights of his day, who were often slow, robotic, and upright. The 6-1, 188-pound Dempsey was a vicious whirling dervish in the ring, always coming forward, bobbing and weaving under punches, and countering with short, swift left hooks and soul-crushing straight rights. It was a style that had never been seen before in a heavyweight, although in later years it would be adopted by such greats as Joe Frazier, Roberto Duran, and Mike Tyson.

Willard met Dempsey on July 4, 1919, in Toledo, Ohio, a match the public roundly expected the much bigger champion to win easily. But although outweighed by nearly 60 pounds, Dempsey gave Willard a brutal beating, flooring him seven times in the first round, inflicting severe facial injuries, and claiming the title when Willard remained on his stool at the start of the fourth round.

That began a seven-year reign as heavyweight champion, during which four of Dempsey's fights generated more than a million dollars at the gate, an unprecedented sum at the time. One of them, his second fight against Gene Tunney, drew boxing's first $2 million gate. Dempsey's fights routinely sold out stadiums seating 75,000, 80,000, and even 100,000 people. In addition to the Willard fight, considered by many to be the most one-sided beating ever administered by a challenger to a reigning heavyweight champion, Dempsey was a central figure in two of the most spectacular bouts in heavyweight history.

In 1923, Dempsey was punched clear out of the ring by Argentine challenger Luis Angel Firpo in the first round of a bout at the Polo Grounds in New York City. He climbed back in to knock Firpo out in the second round, but had been hit so hard he had no recollection of the bout and, in fact, thought he had lost.

In 1926, having taken three years off after marrying an actress and indulging in the pleasures of worldwide celebrity, Dempsey lost his title to Gene Tunney, a mobile boxer in the mold of Corbett and, later, Ali. Their return bout, held a year later, yielded one of the most memorable and controversial moments in boxing history, the so-called Long Count. Having lost the first six rounds of the bout, Dempsey finally cornered Tunney in round 7 and floored him with a lightning-fast flurry of lefts and right. But in the heat of battle, Dempsey refused to abide by a new rule requiring a fighter scoring a knockdown to retreat to a neutral corner to give his opponent a chance to rise. As a result, the referee delayed starting his 10-count over Tunney for anywhere between 5 and 10 seconds, affording the dazed champion sufficient time to recover and beat the count. The argument over how long Tunney was actually on the canvas and whether he could have beaten a normal 10-count is still debated by boxing fans nearly a century later. Tunney went on to win the fight by decision.

Joe Louis and the Resurgence of Heavyweight Boxing

The end of Dempsey's reign ushered in a period of doldrums for the heavyweight division. Tunney retired after making one more title defense, and for the next nine years the title ping-ponged among the likes of skilled but largely nondescript heavyweights such as Max Schmeling, Jack Sharkey, Primo Carnera, Max Baer, and Jim Braddock, immortalized later as the Cinderella Man.

The dullness of the heavyweight division allowed some of the lighter-weight fighters of the era to take center stage, notably Henry Armstrong, who at one time held the lightweight, welterweight, and middleweight titles simultaneously; Barney Ross, a lightweight champion who became a war hero after his career was over, awarded the Silver Star for his service in World War II; lightweight Benny Leonard, a boxer so difficult to hit he would have his hair combed between rounds and come back without a hair out of place; and a bit later, Sugar Ray Robinson, born Walker Smith and widely regarded as the greatest all-around boxer who ever lived. Robinson's career record of 175 wins and 19 defeats, a dozen of which came after his 40th birthday, is one of the greatest accomplishments in professional sports, as is that of former light-heavyweight champion and heavyweight contender Archie Moore, who knocked out an incredible 132 opponents in a career that spanned four decades.

But all of them took a back seat to an unassuming young man from Detroit by way of Alabama named Joe Louis Barrow, who would succeed Jack Johnson as only the second Black heavyweight champion in history. Joe Louis was everything Jack Johnson was not: soft-spoken and humble to the point of being deferential around White people. But his short, stiff punches were lethal in the ring, and his determination to improve himself after being shockingly knocked out by former champion Schmeling after winning his first 24 bouts, all but four by knockout, was demonstrated in one of the most pivotal fights of all time.

A year after knocking out Braddock to win the title, Louis gave Schmeling a rematch at Yankee Stadium. The bout took on international significance because it was 1938, Hitler was running roughshod over Europe, and Schmeling, a

German, was being held up as a symbol of Aryan superiority. So important was the fight that Louis was called to the White House by President Franklin D. Roosevelt, who emphasized the necessity of a Louis victory.

Carrying that pressure into the ring before 70,000 fans at Yankee Stadium, Louis blitzed Schmeling in just over two dramatic minutes of the first round. Later, he would say, "The whole damned country was depending on me." (See Figure 2-4.)

FIGURE 2-4: It took more than 20 years for Joe Louis to become the second Black heavyweight champion of the world.

Carl Van Vechten / Wikimedia Commons / Public domain

Louis held the title for 12 years, longer than any heavyweight champion in history, and defended the title 25 times, a record unmatched by any boxer in any weight class.

Unfortunately, Louis's career came to an ignominious end when, after retiring as champion, he attempted to make a comeback but was convincingly beaten by Ezzard Charles in 1950. Then, in 1951, the final chapter of Louis's career was written when Rocky Marciano, at the time a crude but undefeated young heavyweight, knocked him out in the eighth round at Madison Square Garden, nearly sending him out of the ring with his last punch.

A year later, Marciano would go on to win the title with a spectacular 13th-round knockout of Jersey Joe Walcott, beginning a three-year title reign that would conclude with Marciano as the only heavyweight champion in history to retire with an undefeated record, 49 fights, 49 wins, 43 by knockout. It is a record that remained unmatched until 2015, when Floyd Mayweather Jr. retired after beating Andre

Berto for his 49th win without a loss. Mayweather later defeated Conor McGregor, a UFC fighter making his boxing debut, to claim a record of 50–0.

Marciano was succeeded by Floyd Patterson, a speedy but undersized heavyweight (6-0, around 190 pounds) who not only became history's youngest heavyweight champion (21 years, 10 months) when he defeated Archie Moore for the vacant crown in 1956, but also the first heavyweight to regain the title when he knocked out Ingemar Johansen in 1960. Patterson lost his title for good in 1962 by first-round knockout to Sonny Liston, a fearsome ex-convict who is considered among the hardest punchers in boxing history. Patterson continued to fight as a legitimate title contender for another decade, retiring in 1972 after being stopped in a non-title bout by Muhammad Ali.

Ali: The Greatest — and Loudest — Heavyweight of All

Born Cassius Clay in Louisville, Kentucky on January 17, 1942, the fighter who became Muhammad Ali wasn't deemed to have much chance to beat the dreaded Liston when the two met for the title in Miami Beach on February 25, 1964. Despite having won a gold medal as a light-heavyweight in the 1960 Rome Olympics, young Clay was considered a showboat and a light puncher, faster even with his mouth than with his lightning fists. At the weigh-in on the morning of the Liston fight, Clay became so hysterical that his pulse went up to 220 and the ringside physician threatened to call off the fight, claiming Clay was "scared to death."

But by fight time, Clay was dead calm and methodically picked apart the aging Liston, who surrendered the title on his stool after six rounds, claiming a shoulder injury. (See Figure 2-5.) That fight launched one of the most tumultuous and significant championship reigns in the history of sports. Soon after his victory, Clay announced his conversion to the Nation of Islam and changed his name first to Cassius X, in tribute to Malcolm X, and later to Muhammad Ali. Ali's braggadocio and quick wit made him a polarizing figure among fight fans and the general public and often divided them along racial lines. This was no deferential Joe Louis or judicious Jackie Robinson. The young Ali was a firebrand who made Jack Johnson seem sedate by comparison.

HISTORICAL TIDBIT

Four of the greatest heavyweights of the 1970s celebrated birthdays within two weeks of each other: Floyd Patterson (January 4, 1935), George Foreman (January 10, 1949), Joe Frazier (January 12, 1944), and Muhammad Ali (January 17, 1942).

FIGURE 2-5: Cassius Clay (later Muhammad Ali) stings Sonny Liston with a jab en route to winning the heavyweight crown.

Anonymous / Associated Press

When Ali — having made nine increasingly impressive defenses of his title, including a controversial first round KO of Liston in a rematch — refused to be inducted into the army during the Vietnam War, citing religious objections, he was stripped of his title and his license to box in the United States. As a result, he lost more than three years of his athletic prime before obtaining a license to box in Georgia in October 1970. During that time, Ali scuffled to make a living, earning modest sums as a college lecturer, appearing in a short-lived Broadway show, and receiving financial aid from other boxers, notably Joe Frazier, who would become his most difficult opponent.

HISTORICAL TIDBIT

Ali's exile began the splintering of boxing titles that many blame for the steady decline in the sport's popularity over the past 40 years. In his absence, self-proclaimed "sanctioning organizations" sprang up, such as the World Boxing Association (WBA) and, later, the World Boxing Council (WBC), the International Boxing Federation (IBF), and the World Boxing Organization (WBO), recognizing their own champions and confusing fight fans as to who the "real" champions actually were. At the time of this writing, there were four major boxing organizations with champions in each of 17 weight classes, meaning that as many as 68 boxers could claim themselves to be "world champions."

Ali's exile made him a folk hero to many young fans and members of the 1960s counterculture, and by the time of his 1971 showdown with Frazier, who claimed the title in his absence, Ali had become a symbol of rebellion against the establishment that attracted a huge following. His persona also frightened and repelled many. His bout with Frazier, dubbed "The Fight of the Century," was the biggest sporting event of all time to that point, paying both fighters an unprecedented $2.5 million apiece. The bout generated some $45 million in revenue, mostly through live closed-circuit TV broadcasts in movie theaters, the equivalent of roughly $400 million in 2025 dollars. Although Ali lost a 15-round decision, he gained much respect for his courageous performance.

Three years later, Ali topped himself by defeating George Foreman, the young, strong heavyweight who had dethroned Frazier with a devastating knockout in 1973. As in the first Liston fight, Ali was given virtually no chance to beat Foreman in "The Rumble in the Jungle." But in a masterful performance, Ali dismantled the bigger, stronger, younger man with a risky strategy that became known as the "rope-a-dope" before knocking him cold in the eighth round to regain the title that had been taken from him seven years earlier. It ranks among the greatest comebacks in the history of any sport.

Ali's heroics were still not done. A year later, he met Frazier for a third time, this time as champion, in the fight he named "The Thrilla in Manila." It turned out to be one of the most brutal battles in heavyweight history, with Ali the winner after 14 furious rounds when Frazier's corner would not let him continue due to dangerous swelling that impaired his vision in both eyes.

Over the final three decades of his life, Ali was slowed by Parkinson's disease and eventually lost his ability to speak clearly. His surprise appearance at the 1996 Atlanta Olympics, at which he lit the Olympic cauldron with a trembling hand, was a dramatic and emotional return to public life for Ali after a decade out of the spotlight. He became a beloved figure the world over due to his many philanthropic pursuits and his death in June 2016 at age 74 was mourned by millions, many of whom had disliked and feared him in his prime.

Ali's legacy extended far beyond boxing. His loquacious personality and willingness to taunt his opponents and boast of his skills left an imprint on an entire generation of athletes who followed him; he was the inventor of "trash talk." He also ushered in the era of closed-circuit and pay-per-view television boxing matches due to the financial windfall of his first fight with Frazier, which was viewed globally by a record 300 million viewers and grossed more than $45 million.

As always, Ali had the last word. When he learned how much the fight had grossed compared to the relatively piddling $2.5 million paid to the fighters, he said, "Joe Frazier, we got robbed!"

The Post-Ali Blues

Ali's retirement in 1982 opened the door for many lighter-weight fighters to grab the boxing spotlight. Lightweight Roberto Duran, middleweight Marvelous Marvin Hagler (See Figure 2-6), welterweight Thomas Hearns, and 1976 Olympic gold medalist Ray Leonard all had outstanding careers in the 1970s and 1980s. All benefited by widespread exposure on broadcast television in their lesser bouts, and the emerging gold mine of pay television — first, closed-circuit broadcasts in movie theaters and later, bouts offered by cable television networks on a pay-per-view basis — resulted in multimillion-dollar paychecks that dwarfed those of Ali and Frazier.

The fights between Hagler and Hearns, Leonard and Duran, and ultimately, Hagler and Leonard, were big-money spectacles, often held in Las Vegas casinos, that grabbed the attention not only of boxing aficionados but casual fans as well. Meanwhile, the heavyweight division languished in the absence of Ali.

FIGURE 2-6: Marvin Hagler, who legally changed his first name to Marvelous, held the middleweight title for seven years.

Killer Kowalski / Wikimedia Commons / Public domain

Ali was succeeded by Larry Holmes, who, although an excellent heavyweight champion, lacked both Ali's charisma and the caliber of opposition Ali had faced in Liston, Frazier, and Foreman. Similar to the doldrums that plagued the division after Dempsey's retirement, Holmes's seven-year reign was followed by a succession of nondescript heavyweights passing the title back and forth as if it were the common cold.

Once more, boxing's glamour division was in a holding pattern.

Kid Dynamite: The Rise of Mike Tyson

In 1984, the boxing headlines were dominated not only by outstanding lighter-weight fighters such as Sugar Ray Leonard, Thomas Hearns, Marvelous Marvin Hagler, and Roberto Duran, but also by a group of nine young American boxers who had won gold medals at the Los Angeles Olympics, notably Meldrick Taylor, Pernell Whitaker, Mark Breland, and Tyrell Biggs. All would go on to have significant pro careers, although none would be as prominent as a tenth American, light-heavyweight Evander Holyfield, who had to settle for bronze after being controversially disqualified in a semifinal bout for hitting his opponent on a break. Ultimately, Holyfield would be a key figure in some of the most memorable bouts of the 1990s.

And at the same time, a fighter who failed to qualify for the 1984 Olympic team was quietly amassing a résumé that would relegate all of them to the background, at least temporarily. His name was Mike Tyson. (See Figure 2-7.)

Tyson, a heavyweight, had lost in the Olympic trials to Henry Tillman, who would go on to win a gold medal in Los Angeles. A few months after the Olympics, Tyson turned pro with a first-round knockout of one Hector Merced. That victory began a run of 19 consecutive KO victories, some frighteningly violent, which began to attract the attention of the boxing world.

In addition to his impressive hand speed and devastating punching power, Tyson had a compelling backstory. Growing up largely unsupervised in Brooklyn's tough Bedford-Stuyvesant neighborhood, Tyson was remanded to an upstate institution for juvenile delinquents as a 12-year-old. There, he took up boxing and soon caught the attention of Cus D'Amato, the legendary and reclusive trainer/manager of former heavyweight champion Floyd Patterson, among other notable fighters. The narrative of "Cus and the Kid" struck a chord with boxing fans and the general public alike, and Tyson fights became a staple of Saturday afternoon network boxing.

On November 22, 1986, Tyson, at 20 years and five months old, became the youngest heavyweight champion in boxing history, with a second-round KO of Trevor Berbick, to claim the WBC version of the title. Five months later, Tyson added the WBA title with a decision over James Smith, and three months after that he defeated IBF champion Tony Tucker to become the first heavyweight to own all three belts. The following June, Tyson demolished Michael Spinks in 91 seconds in one of the most highly anticipated heavyweight title bouts in years. His popularity and earnings were at an all-time high.

FIGURE 2-7: Twenty-year-old Mike Tyson on the verge of becoming the youngest heavyweight champion in history.

Roy London / Wikimedia Commons / Public domain

But soon afterward, Tyson's career and reputation began to unravel. His marriage to actress Robin Givens ended amid allegations of domestic violence. In February 1990, he lost his title to James (Buster) Douglas in a shocking upset. And two years later, Tyson was convicted of the rape of a teenaged beauty pageant contestant and spent three years in prison.

In Tyson's absence, several fighters rose to the forefront, notably Whitaker, Holyfield, Riddick Bowe, and Mexican lightweight Julio Cesar Chavez. But none provided the drama of 45-year-old George Foreman, who had lost his title 20 years earlier to Muhammad Ali and did not fight for more than a decade, shocking the world by knocking out 25-year-old Michael Moorer to regain the crown in April 1994. Wearing the same red trunks he had worn the night he lost to Ali, Foreman lost every round of the fight before knocking Moorer unconscious with a single right hand in the 10th round.

Although Tyson was released from prison in February 1995 and regained a portion of the heavyweight title a few months later with a stoppage of England's Frank Bruno, he was never the same fighter. In November 1996 he was soundly beaten by Evander Holyfield, and in their rematch eight months later, Tyson was disqualified for biting off a portion of Holyfield's ear. That transgression cost Tyson his license to box for 18 months. When he returned to action, Tyson faced nondescript opposition before challenging heavyweight champion Lennox Lewis in May 2002. The 35-year-old Tyson was brutally KO'd in eight rounds by Lewis and went on to lose two of his next three fights, including stoppages by journeymen Danny Williams and Kevin McBride.

Tyson retired after the McBride loss but returned to the ring in 2020, at 54, to face former multiple champion and Olympic gold medalist Roy Jones Jr. in an eight-round bout that was scored a draw. Five years later, Tyson returned again, and was beaten in a desultory performance by Jake Paul, a YouTube personality who had recently taken up boxing.

As a result, Tyson left a muddled legacy — a fierce puncher and true phenomenon of the 1980s, but also a fighter who was unable to sustain his level of performance against top-flight opposition. His final record of 50 wins and seven losses, five of them by knockout and three to very questionable opposition — is a mixed bag at best.

The Pay-Per-View Champions

While Tyson's star was fading in the mid-1990s, several lower-weight-class fighters were on the ascent, as was boxing on pay-per-view (PPV) television, which allowed boxing fans to purchase major fights and watch them at home on their TV sets. Tyson was the first real PPV star; eight of his bouts — seven of which took place after his release from prison — generated some $800 million in TV revenue. That paved the way for PPV windfalls for several lighter-weight boxers.

Oscar De la Hoya

Oscar de la Hoya, a gold medalist at the 1992 Barcelona Olympics, won the first of his 11 world titles in six weight classes in 1994, and his good looks and Mexican American heritage made him immensely popular, particularly with West Coast fight fans (de la Hoya grew up in East Los Angeles). (See Figure 2-8.) His bouts with Felix Trinidad, Floyd Mayweather Jr., and Manny Pacquiao generated approximately $350 million in PPV revenue.

Manny Pacquiao

Pacquiao, a dynamic Filipino boxer-puncher who began fighting as a 106-pounder in 1995, eventually won titles in eight weight classes, including welterweight (147 pounds). (See Figure 2-9.) His 2015 showdown with Mayweather Jr. attracted a record 4.6 million PPV buys and generated an unprecedented half-billion dollars in revenue. Overall, Pacquiao's bouts attracted an estimated 20 million PPV buys and approximately $1.3 billion in revenue.

FIGURE 2-8: Oscar de la Hoya's good looks and Olympic gold medal made him a superstar of '80s and '90s boxing.

James Devaney/Getty Images

FIGURE 2-9: Manny Pacquiao's popularity was so great that the Philippines issued a stamp in his honor.

Philippine Postal Corporation / Wikimedia Commons / Public domain

Floyd Mayweather Jr.

Mayweather Jr., who nicknamed himself "Money" and shrewdly marketed himself as a pro wrestling-type "heel," parlayed his bad boy image into twice being named the highest-paid athlete in the world by *Forbes* magazine, in 2014 and 2015. (See Figure 2-10.) His revenue-generating ability surpassed even that of Pacquiao, attracting some 24 million PPV buys and $1.67 billion in gross revenue.

With his victory over Andre Berto in 2015, Mayweather matched Rocky Marciano's achievement of 49 victories without a defeat, after which he retired. He returned to the ring in 2017 to fight Conor McGregor, a mixed-martial arts fighter who had never had a boxing match. Mayweather's TKO victory gave him a record of 50–0, surpassing Marciano's record by one win. Mayweather's quick hands, watertight defense, and astronomical boxing IQ earned a ranking of number three on the list of all-time great boxers by the record-keeping website BoxRec.com.

FIGURE 2-10: The never-beaten (50–0) Floyd Mayweather Jr. in the process of defeating Juan Manuel Marquez.

MARK RALSTON/Getty Images

Canelo Alvarez

Saul (Canelo) Alvarez, a Mexican boxer who won titles in divisions ranging from junior middleweight (154 pounds) to light-heavyweight (175), in 2018 signed the most lucrative contract ever given to a professional athlete, $365 million for 11 bouts over a five-year period. (See Figure 2-11.) The contract was with DAZN, a PPV-outlet that charged its subscribers a monthly fee that entitled them to unlimited access to its offerings. But the deal fell apart after just four bouts, with Alvarez claiming breach of contract. He fought a dozen more times after splitting with DAZN, including a victory in the final bout of his trilogy with former middleweight champion Gennadiy Golovkin, but lost his highest-profile bout, by decision to Terence Crawford, a welterweight and junior-middleweight champion jumping up to 168, in September 2025.

FIGURE 2-11: Saul (Canelo) Alvarez, a champion in four weight classes, signed history's most lucrative sports contract in 2018.

Tom Hogan/Getty Images

Whither the Heavyweights?

Following the retirement of Lennox Lewis in 2002, the heavyweights once again went through a period in which the title was passed back and forth like a hot potato among a succession of boxers of varying skills. No fewer than 27 boxers claimed to own a part of the World Heavyweight Championship over the next two decades, thanks to the existence of four sanctioning organizations, each of which recognized its own champion. The best of these was likely Wladmir Klitschko, who defended his portion of the title 20 times over 10 years before he was beaten in back-to-back fights by Tyson Fury and Anthony Joshua.

But no fighter could claim to be undisputed heavyweight champion of the world until Oleksandr Usyk, a well-schooled and highly trained Ukrainian heavyweight, knocked out Daniel Dubois in July 2025. With that victory, Usyk — who had already defeated Fury and Joshua — became the first undisputed heavyweight champion in a quarter-century.

In an age of super heavyweights, Usyk's comparatively "small" physique — 6-3 and around 220 pounds — is a throwback to the days when the heavyweight champion need not be the biggest man on the planet, merely the best fighter.

Woman Warriors: From Christy Martin to Claressa Shields

Although there are accounts of women engaging in boxing matches as far back as the 18th century, it was not until the 1990s that women's boxing became a viable sport. In fact, it was illegal for two women to box in most jurisdictions around the world until the second half of the 20th century. The first woman to be issued a boxing license in the United States was Caroline Svendsen, who was licensed by the state of Nevada in 1975. It took more than two decades longer in the UK, when Jane Couch was issued a license in 1998 by the British Boxing Board of Control after a long legal battle. Couch went on to win a professional world championship in her fifth professional fight and was inducted into the International Boxing Hall of Fame in 2024. (See Figure 2-12.)

FIGURE 2-12: Jane Couch, the first woman licensed to box in the United Kingdom, won a title in her fifth pro fight.

Jed Jacobsohn / Getty Images

By the 1990s, women's boxing had become not only accepted, but a staple of major boxing events, spearheaded by the signing of Christy Martin with Don King Promotions in 1993. Martin, billed as "The Coal Miner's Daughter," was given featured spots on the undercards of several title bouts headlined by men, including both heavyweight title fights between Evander Holyfield and Mike Tyson. Martin's spectacular win over Ireland's Deirdre Gogarty in 1996 resulted in her becoming the first female boxer featured on the cover of *Sports Illustrated*. (See Figure 2-13.) In 2020, Martin was the first woman inducted into the International Boxing Hall of Fame in Canastota, New York.

FIGURE 2-13: Christy Martin, seen here defeating Diedre Gogarty in 1996, was the first female boxer featured on the cover of *Sports Illustrated*.

Al Bello / Getty Images

Martin's success boosted the popularity of women's boxing, luring the likes of Laila Ali, daughter of Muhammad Ali, and Jacqueline Frazier-Lyde, daughter of Joe Frazier, into the professional ring. Other notable female boxers of the era include Lucia Rijker of the Netherlands, Cecilia Braekhus of Norway, and Mexican-American Mia St. John.

At the time of this writing, Katie Taylor of Ireland, winner of 25 out of 26 bouts and a two-division world champion, is probably the world's best-known and highest-paid female boxer. Her three bouts with American Amanda Serrano are the women's equivalent of the legendary Ali-Frazier trilogy for ferocity and competitiveness. The third bout between Taylor and Serrano, won by Taylor, headlined an all-female card that sold out New York City's Madison Square Garden in July 2025.

Claressa Shields of Flint, Michigan, has been a champion in both the middleweight and heavyweight divisions and was unbeaten in her first 17 bouts. Shields also holds another distinction: She is the last American boxer to have won an Olympic gold medal, and the only US boxer in history to have won the gold in back-to-back Olympics, at the 2012 London Games and the 2016 Rio de Janeiro Games. (See Figure 2-14.) No US male boxer has won an Olympic gold medal since Andre Ward in 2004.

FIGURE 2-14: In addition to being a professional world champion, Claressa Shields, here defeating Danielle Perkins in 2025, is the most recent American boxer to win an Olympic gold medal.

Nic Antaya / Getty Images

Despite the growing popularity of women's boxing, the gender gap in pay between men and women boxers is significant. In 2018, Katie Taylor was the world's highest-paid female boxer, earning $1 million. The same year, her male counterpart, Tyson Fury, earned $57 million.

There are also significant rule differences between men's and women's boxing. Whereas men fight three-minute rounds and their championship bouts are scheduled for 12 rounds, women are limited to 10 rounds of no longer than two minutes. And while there are now 17 weight divisions in male boxing, female boxing consists of 13 divisions, ranging from pinweight (no more than 101 pounds) to heavyweight (over 189).

IN THIS CHAPTER

» Building a boxer's body

» Attaining the stamina to go the distance

» Realizing your true capabilities

» Defying the perceived limits of age

Chapter 3
Changing Your Body and Mind with a Boxing Workout

Boxing training offers many more benefits than simply learning to deliver a powerful punch. Applied diligently, a boxing program transforms the way you look, the way you feel, and even the way you think. It takes a special mindset to withstand the rigors of boxing training and to take your newfound skills to the next level. I have had parents tell me that boxing training improved their teenager's self-confidence, and senior citizen clients who told me that boxing training actually changed their lives.

And the interesting thing is that many of my most dedicated clients tell me that before they started boxing training, they were a bit intimidated by the thought of trying a workout that involved punching and, they believed, attracted a frightening element to the gym. Instead, they have discovered that at the entry level, boxing is a community based on mutual respect and encouragement. And the physical benefits are many.

If you dedicate yourself to a consistent boxing training routine, I can guarantee you several things:

- You will get stronger without becoming overly muscular.
- You will get leaner without feeling emaciated or sucked down.
- You will have improved cardio function, both aerobically and anaerobically, because an intense boxing workout demands both.
- You will feel better about yourself than you have in years, because boxing is not only a workout, but a skill set and a mindset that you will be proud to have mastered.

Having Shoulders and a Core to Die For

Since boxing involves a coordinated movement of the kinetic chain — that is, the dynamic interaction of your feet, legs, hips, core, shoulders, arms and finally, fists — a boxing workout is by its very nature going to develop and strengthen all those parts of your body. Most of the work, however, is done by your hips, core, and shoulders, and that is where you will see most of the changes to your body. A consistent punching workout will give you shoulder caps that look like a small bunch of bananas and a torso that tapers down to a pair of slim but powerful hips. And you might just develop that six-pack you always dreamed of.

Going 15 Rounds? No Problem!

At its essence, boxing is a HIIT workout — High-Intensity Interval Training. That's because you work in segments of three minutes of exertion to one minute of rest. You bounce between periods of *anaerobic* activity — times when you are working so hard that you cannot comfortably speak — with periods of aerobic activity, where you are still breathing deeply, but more comfortably. And after a time, you will find that the one-minute rest period is more than sufficient to get you ready for the next round.

Not going to lie — it will be difficult at first. Many of my clients found it impossible to work for an entire three-minute round, or to work two rounds in a row. That's fine; I often start out new clients with one-minute rounds followed by 20 seconds of rest. But after a couple of weeks of this, they find it easy to graduate to full-length rounds and eventually 10, 12, or even 15 of them in a row. Aerobic capacity and cardiac function are among the most responsive to boxing training, and you'll be surprised at how quickly they improve with consistent workouts.

Keeping the Psychological Benefits in Mind: Poise and Self-Confidence in Abundance

Many of my clients came to their first class with a sense of trepidation. Some were intimidated by the thought of boxing as something indulged in by scary characters. Others had an understandable aversion to violence and thought the workout involved hitting someone else or, worse, getting hit themselves. Still others thought the techniques of boxing would be too difficult for them to learn.

What most of them found out was that a boxing workout need not be frightening or violent or especially difficult. It does take a fair amount of patience to do it right, because many of the movements, especially using your nondominant hand in such a prominent fashion, can be challenging. But the learning and mastering of even a couple of punches — the basic jab and cross, for instance — imparts a level of satisfaction that few other workouts can offer. Let's face it, we all know how to walk or run on a treadmill and it only takes a few minutes of instruction to learn how to use a weight machine or lift a barbell. But mastering the moves used in boxing is more like taking a dance class. Difficult, yes, but incredibly gratifying when you get it down. And, invariably, with that comes a boost in confidence and self-reliance that is an added benefit of the boxing workout.

You're Never Too Old — or Too Young

One of the most common objections I hear from new clients is that they are "too old" to start boxing training. And yet I have had clients as old as 90 and as young as 12. Boxing workouts have been scientifically shown to increase bone density, improve cardiac fitness, and benefit mobility disorders. Boxing is one of the main forms of exercise prescribed for sufferers of Parkinson's disease and the Rock Steady Boxing program designed to improve the movement of Parkinson's patients has taken off across the country. In a lot of cases, the people who were the most reluctant to try boxing have become its most devoted participants. I have had clients tell me they're now "addicted" to their boxing workouts, and many have invested in their own heavy and speed bags for workouts in between our four-days-a-week classes.

I have trained septuagenarians who had boxed a bit in their youth and youths who have been bullied at school, were too small for other sports, or simply wanted to try something new. There is no limit to who can benefit from a boxing workout other than the limits we put upon ourselves.

Training Like a Fighter

There's an old saying in boxing: "You will fight the way you train," and truer words were never spoken. Since human beings are by nature creatures of habit, bad habits developed in the gym will inevitably transfer themselves to the ring. A boxer who is accustomed to cutting corners in workouts or on the road will naturally fall into the same pattern during a fight. That's why it's important to train as intensely in the gym as if it were fight night. Also, for those who have no intention of actually stepping into the ring, it's the best way to achieve the tip-top conditioning of a professional boxer.

So how do we start? Like any good construction project, we go from the ground up. And that means at the legs.

Hitting the Road

Roadwork, or what we now call running, has been a linchpin of boxing training going back to the 18th century. In those days, it was not uncommon to find (probably apocryphal) accounts of boxers running up to 20 miles while chained to a horse-drawn wagon! It was customary for boxers to run in heavy work boots and to incorporate such exercises as performing chin-ups on the branch of a tree or playing leapfrog with their road companions during the course of a run.

Thankfully, that way of thinking has changed, but the basic concept hasn't. Long-distance running is still considered essential for the aerobic and anaerobic fitness necessary for an intense boxing workout. An old rule of thumb stated that the boxer should run for as long as the scheduled length of their bout. For example, for a four-round fight, lasting 15 minutes with rest periods, 15 minutes of running would be sufficient. For a 15-round bout, the run would be 59 minutes.

These days, the general guideline for superior aerobic fitness calls for between 75 and 150 minutes of intense cardio training per week. I tend to favor the latter number, which means a run of about a half-hour five days per week.

In recent years, fighters have also incorporated sprints and plyometric-type training into their roadwork sessions, and it makes a lot of sense. *Plyometric* training, also known as *explosive* training, involves short bursts of intense activity, such as jumping on and off of platforms ranging from 12 inches in height to three feet and more, to generate explosive power. Since boxing is performed in intense three-minute blocks with one-minute rest periods, it stands to reason that an effective form of roadwork would consist of a series of three-minute sprints, or close to it, with 60 seconds of rest in between. And since effective boxing involves the explosive movement of punching, it is clear why plyometric-type training would be beneficial to boxers. Former heavyweight champion Evander Holyfield was an early proponent of both sprinting and plyometric training during the 1990s and his superb conditioning carried him through many grueling bouts.

So when should you run? Traditionally, fighters were forced to run at the crack of dawn, a rule that never made much sense to me. After all, most professional boxing matches take place in the evening. Why train the body to work hard at a time when the fighter should be resting?

A famous trainer once explained the reasoning to me thus: "It's to force the fighter to do something he really doesn't want to do, because the odds are that in a fight, there will come a time when he has to do something he really doesn't want to do, and this prepares him mentally for that moment."

Understood. But for the rest of us, who are probably not training for an actual fight (and, if you're like me, pretty useless physically in the early morning), the run should be performed whenever it is most convenient and feels right to you. The important thing is to do it on a consistent basis, and to try to enjoy it, not make it a chore that you dread having to do.

It's OK, in fact essential, that you wear proper running shoes for your roadwork — *no* work boots or boxing shoes — and you needn't do it outside, especially in winter or severe heat. Running on a treadmill is perfectly fine.

Seeing Discipline as the Key to Success

As in all endeavors, physical or mental, consistency of effort is important, and that takes some discipline. All of us on some days will be tempted just to go through the motions in a workout, but the one way to ensure the success of any workout program is to give all you've got every single time.

That doesn't mean that you'll be able to run as fast or lift as much or spar as well in every single workout; the human body doesn't work that way. There will be days when you simply can't run that seven-minute mile or squat with those 315 pounds on your back or throw 200 punches a round in a heavy bag workout.

What it does mean is that every time out, you will give the best effort you have on that day and leave no crumbs on the table. It means not running an eight-minute mile on a day when you're capable of running a seven-minute mile. It means not squatting 250 pounds when you feel strong enough to do 315. And it means not throwing 150 punches on a day when you could physically throw 200.

It means using what you've got in the tank right now, not saving it for tomorrow. Although your performance may not be the same at every workout, your effort should be. And that takes discipline.

Setting Aside Gym Time as Sacred

Along those same lines, it is imperative that nothing short of an emergency get in the way of your gym time if you want to achieve optimal fitness. This is especially true in boxing workouts, where skills are honed through repetition. If you are tired or injured, taking a day off here and there can be beneficial, but simply skipping gym sessions because you "don't feel like it" will set you back. Champion boxers train through holidays, weekends, minor illnesses, and injuries because they know how detrimental an unnecessary day off can be to their training schedule. You are probably not training for a fight, but presumably you are training to achieve superior fitness, and for that the workout must be your religion and the gym your house of worship.

A typical boxing workout is described in detail in Chapter 14, but plan on five days of running per week and at least three days in the gym, with a 60- to 90-minute workout consisting of stretching, warmup, 10–12 rounds of bag punching, and mitt work, followed by some strength and core training and cooldown.

2 The Tools of the Trade

IN THIS PART . . .

Learn the difference between speed bag gloves, heavy bag gloves, and fight gloves, and why boxers choose one type of glove to hit the smaller, faster bags and another type to hit the sometimes unforgiving heavy bags.

Wrap your hands correctly to protect your knuckles and stabilize your wrists, and the difference between standard hand wraps and the ready-made variety.

Find out about the different varieties of boxing shoes and what they offer you in terms of comfort, support, traction, and price.

Learn to choose and properly fit a boxing mouthguard, another essential bit of equipment no boxer should ever be without.

Select the perfect ring outfit for when you make your dramatic entrance into the arena.

IN THIS CHAPTER

» Choosing the right gloves

» Choosing the right shoes

» Choosing the right trunks, robe, and socks

Chapter 4 Dressing for Success

When I was starting out as a young amateur boxer, an older fighter said to me, "If you dress like a champion, you'll fight like a champion."

This turned out not to be entirely the case, but the point was well-taken. As in any serious pursuit, the look and quality of your equipment will go a long way to determine the success of your endeavor. As such it is important that you choose your gear carefully, with an eye on function and durability rather than looks. Picking the right gloves and shoes is vital not only for the effectiveness of your workouts but also for the avoidance of injury. And while any workout clothes will suffice for gym time, it's always fun to pick out a sharp-looking ring outfit if you decide eventually to climb into the ring for real.

Choose Your Weapons: Gloves

Let's establish one thing right off the bat: Boxing gloves were invented to protect the fighter who is punching, not the one who is getting punched. The skull is the hardest part of the human body, and the unprotected human hand was not designed to crash into it repeatedly. Something's gotta give, and it's usually a wrist, a knuckle, or a metacarpal. One of the main complaints about boxing in the bareknuckle era was that it was difficult, and painful, for boxers to hit one another continually, which is why fights routinely lasted for hours, and often featured long periods with more grappling than punching. The padded boxing glove, introduced at the end of the 19th century, was intended not to cushion blows against a boxer's skull, but to save the hands from injury, allowing more and harder punching. The familiar expression "Take the gloves off" to signify when things are about to get rough is actually a misnomer, because a boxer can do a lot more damage with the gloves on.

As a beginning boxer, you should know that there are four distinct types of boxing gloves: two for hitting bags, one for sparring, and one for fights. Let's take a look at the differences.

Bag gloves I: For hitting the speed bag

There are actually two different types of bag gloves, one for hitting the speed bag and the other for hitting the heavy, double-end and cobra-type bags. Most boxers prefer to use a smaller, lighter glove when hitting the speed bag, although some prefer to use no gloves at all, merely hand wraps. (Hand-wrapping, another essential protective measure, is covered in detail in Chapter 5.) Generally, speed bag gloves have minimal padding and have elastic at the wrist to keep them tight. (See Figure 4-1.) The reason for this is twofold: For one thing, as its name implies, the speed bag moves fast and it is difficult, if not impossible, to keep up with it while wearing a full-sized boxing glove. For another, being able to feel the speed bag through your gloves is important to hit it effectively, and a light glove or hand wrap allows a boxer to do that. You can get a good pair of these "old-school" gloves for between $30 and $50.

FIGURE 4-1: Light leather gloves are perfect for hitting the speed bag.

Courtesy of TITLE Boxing

Bag gloves II: For hitting the heavy, double-end, and cobra bags

Hitting these bags requires a bit more padding at the knuckles, which is why most boxers prefer to hit them with gloves that are larger than fight gloves. (See Figure 4-2.) These gloves generally weigh between 12 and 16 ounces, and most are secured with Velcro straps around the wrist, allowing the boxer to put them on and take them off without assistance, which of course is essential if you are training alone. Most heavyweights and boxers with larger hands will opt for 16-ounce gloves, because it is difficult and uncomfortable to squeeze a large, wrapped fist into a smaller glove. Women with smaller hands will do just fine with 12- or 14-ounce gloves. Although nowadays "synthetic" leathers are much improved from the days when budget gloves were made of vinyl, opt for genuine leather gloves. They will last longer and mold to your hands over time, resulting in a much more comfortable workout.

Because the heavy bag is essentially a stationary target, you need not worry about keeping up with it as you would the speed bag, and because most heavy bags (with the exception of water-filled models) provide a stiff resistance, it is imperative that you wear a well-padded glove when hitting them.

It's possible to hit the double-end bag with speed bag gloves or even hand wraps, but using the heavier gloves on it will improve your hand speed, much the way swinging a leaded bat will improve a baseball player's bat speed when hitting in a game. Cobra-style bags, which are a durable foam ball mounted on a spring atop a pole, are significantly harder than air-filled double-end bags and should only be hit with wraps and the same gloves you use on the heavy bag.

FIGURE 4-2: More heavily padded gloves, weighing between 12 and 16 ounces, are suitable for the heavy bag and sparring.

Courtesy of TITLE Boxing

In earlier times gloves were stuffed with horsehair, but nowadays most are filled with either foam rubber or some sort of gel, which makes for a longer-lasting glove. Expect to spend between $50 and $250 on a good pair of bag gloves.

Sparring gloves

When and if you do climb into the ring to spar, it will be with gloves similar to those you use on the heavy bag. Many heavy bag gloves are perfectly suitable for sparring. In fact, many gyms will not allow you to spar with anything smaller than 16-ounce gloves, because the extra weight blunts the impact of punches and is safer to use in what should be a noncompetitive learning environment. Gloves made specifically for sparring are often lace-up style, which provides a tighter, more secure fit than Velcro, but as mentioned above, these require a second person to do the tying. Once again, go with genuine leather for long life and superior comfort. A good pair of sparring gloves will run you about $100.

Fight gloves

If you get to the point where you're ready for actual competition, you'll be supplied with a pair of fight gloves, which are different again from bag or sparring gloves. In amateur competitions, glove sizes will range from 8 to 12 ounces, depending upon weight class. The pros specify 8-ounce gloves for all weight classes up to welterweight (147 pounds), and 10-ounce gloves for all higher weight classes. The smaller gloves ensure a faster-paced fight and more knockouts because there is less padding over the knuckles. Fight gloves are always laced up and the knot at the wrist is wrapped with white adhesive tape to help them remain tied and prevent a fighter from using the laces to injure an opponent. (See Figure 4-3.)

The gloves are supplied by the promoter at the pre-fight weigh-in, and in championship fights the principles will be allowed to select the actual pair to be used in the fight, as well as a backup pair in case of a glove failure during the bout. In a previous era, both fighters were required to wear the same brand and color of gloves, but nowadays fighters are permitted to select whatever brand and color they prefer as long as they are made by a commission-approved manufacturer and are of the correct weight.

Fight gloves for amateur competitions, including the Olympic Games, weigh 10 ounces and have a white band across the knuckles, which designates the scoring area. If the white area of the glove does not make contact with the opponent's body, the judges are not permitted to credit it as a scoring blow.

FIGURE 4-3: Fight gloves are smaller (8 to 10 ounces) and laced for a more secure fit.

Courtesy of TITLE Boxing

Finding the Perfect Shoes for Your Fancy Footwork

They say baseball is a game of inches. Boxing is a game of feet — specifically, where you place them and how you move them around the ring. We discuss boxing footwork in detail in Chapter 10, but before we get to that, let's talk about what you should be wearing on your dogs when you step into the ring.

High-tops or low?

Boxing shoes generally come in three iterations: high-tops, midrange, and low-tops. Each has its own assets and drawbacks, and your choice will largely depend upon your personal preference. High-top boxing shoes (see Figure 4-4) provide the most ankle support, which is important when pushing hard off the balls of your feet and pivoting on your toes to generate extra power. But some find them heavy and uncomfortable, and they can be a pain to get on and off because the laces have to be loosened all the way down the foot. High-top boxing shoes come up approximately 12 inches, or about mid-calf on most individuals. They run from $50 to $150.

FIGURE 4-4: High-top boxing shoes generally come up to about mid-calf.

Courtesy of TITLE Boxing

Low-top boxing shoes (see Figure 4-5) are similar to basketball or running shoes in style, but much lighter and without the ankle support provided by high-tops. They're great if you want to be able to skitter lightly around the ring but they do present the unwelcome possibility of rolling an ankle in the middle of a fight or sparring session, which is not what you want. You can get a decent pair of low-tops for about $80.

FIGURE 4-5: Low-top boxing shoes come up barely higher than basket-ball shoes.

Courtesy of TITLE Boxing

Personally, I prefer a midrange type of shoe, about seven inches high, which provides sufficient ankle support without the added weight and stiffness of a high-top shoe, as shown in Figure 4-6. A good pair can be had for between $40 and $120.

FIGURE 4-6: Mid-top shoes provide the best of both worlds.

Courtesy of TITLE Boxing

Rubber-soled or leather?

No need to make a choice on this anymore.

Back in "the day," and even when I was boxing competitively in the 1970s, most boxing shoes had leather soles, presumably to reduce weight. These soles were smooth and often slippery, and before a fight you would see trainers scraping the bottoms of their boxers' shoes with a serrated knife to rough up the surface and provide better traction.

In those days, one neutral corner of the ring had a resin box for the fighters to step into to improve traction, but this is no longer permitted or necessary.

Today's boxing shoes almost all come equipped with rubber soles, textured enough to allow a fighter to dig into the canvas while remaining light enough to permit smooth and swift movement around the ring.

Nylon mesh or leather?

Again, a matter of personal preference. Genuine leather boxing shoes are more durable than nylon mesh. They are also pricier and not as breathable, meaning your feet can get awfully hot inside them over the course of a tough fight or sparring session. A good-quality pair of leather boxing shoes will almost always cost you over 100 bucks.

Nylon mesh is a good alternative because these shoes are lighter and allow your feet to breathe, as well as being less expensive. They are not as durable as leather shoes, of course, as anyone who runs regularly in mesh running shoes can attest. Currently, I train in a pair of mesh midrange shoes that cost $40 and have held up well for over a year of intense training sessions.

As a third alternative, there are shoes made of "synthetic leather," usually a form of plastic such as PVC or polyurethane applied over a paper or microfiber backing. This is less expensive than real leather and, according to some manufacturers, requires less maintenance. Several boxing equipment manufacturers offer synthetic leather shoes for between $50 and $70.

Complete the Look: Trunks, Robes, and Socks

One of the great things about boxing is that it allows its athletes to wear a uniform of their own choosing, in whichever colors or styles they prefer. Boxing is not a team sport, so unless you're fighting in an international competition or representing a particular gym in an amateur tournament, you're free to choose from a variety of styles, colors, and materials. Traditionally, boxing trunks and robes were made of satin, but some boxers opted for a velour-like material. And some, such as Hector (Macho) Camacho, preferred to come into the ring in a modified loincloth. Former world champion Jorge Paez once even came into the ring in a wedding gown.

You can find professional quality boxing trunks (see Figure 4-7) for between $20 and $40, and robes (see Figure 4-8) — which come in full and three-quarter lengths — for about 50 bucks. Be sure to have your name, and nickname, if any, emblazoned across the back. Remember, if you're an amateur boxer, you'll also wear a singlet (a tank top–type shirt), and these are readily available for less than $20. If you really want to look sharp, make sure your corner people are decked out in similar colors bearing your name as well.

The choice of socks is up to you. Mike Tyson famously came into the ring wearing no socks under his boxing shoes, but you'll likely find it preferable to wear them, if only to prevent blisters and foul-smelling shoes. Some boxers like the socks to rise up considerably higher than their boxing shoes. Others prefer to show no more than an inch or so. Again, back in "the day," many fighters rolled their socks down to the top of their shoes; you see this in any photo of Jack Dempsey in the ring. Again, the right choice is whatever is comfortable to you.

FIGURE 4-7: Traditional boxing trunks.

Courtesy of TITLE Boxing

FIGURE 4-8: A satin robe completes the look.

Courtesy of TITLE Boxing

IN THIS CHAPTER

» Protecting your hands

» Protecting your head

» Protecting your body

» Protecting your teeth and jaw

Chapter 5

Keeping the Damage to a Minimum

At risk of repeating myself, let me say that boxing is inherently dangerous and not only because of the damage that can occur from punches to the head. The hands must also be protected, as well as the teeth, the jaw, the groin, and, especially for women, the chest area. A wide array of protective gear is essential for avoiding injury, even if your workouts never stray from your basement gymnasium.

Practicing the Fine Art of Hand Wrapping

A lot of new clients ask me, "If we're already wearing gloves, why do we have to wrap our hands?" Many of them find hand wrapping to be time-consuming and difficult to do correctly, and many are under the mistaken impression that the padding of the gloves alone is enough to ensure a safe workout.

In truth, the gloves really only protect your knuckles. Properly applied hand wraps protect everything else. And you must remember that as a boxer, your hands are your most important body part, every bit as vital to your success as they are to a surgeon's or a pianist's. So it's worth it to take a few minutes to learn how to wrap your hands correctly and to do it before every workout.

Mastering basic wrapping

There are as many ways to wrap a boxer's hands as there are fingers on both of them. And there is no actual "correct" way to do it. Basically, what you want to do when wrapping your hands is provide support to your wrist, which is prone to injury if the fist is loose on impact, especially when throwing a hook, and to keep the metacarpals (the five long bones between the wrist and fingers) from spreading on contact with a firm object. I find that a 180-inch slightly elasticized wrap works best for me and for my clients.

The simplest way to do this is with a basic wrap that begins with two or three winds around the wrist, followed by four or five wraps around the knuckles, a crisscross at the palm, a wind or two around the thumb, a crisscross at the back of the hand, and a fastening at the wrist (as shown in the following illustrations).

All wraps begin the same way, with the loop over the thumb and the wrap pulled backward toward the wrist. And the wrap should be applied firmly, but not too tight. If you cut off the circulation to your hand, you will find yourself removing your glove and loosening the wrap in the middle of the workout — bad idea and big waste of time. And you should heed the message on one side of the wrap (*This side down*) to ensure that the Velcro finishes right side up when you fasten it at the wrist.

Going between the fingers

I prefer to use a slightly more complex wrap for myself and my clients, one that winds between the fingers, creating a secure support for the wrist when the fist is tightened. Refer to the photos in this section to get it right. To perform this wrap, start with the loop over your thumb and pull the wrap backward across the back of your hand, as shown in Figure 5-1. Wind the wrap twice around your wrist, again, firmly but not too tight.

Next, pull the wrap diagonally across the back of your hand and between your little and ring fingers, as shown in Figure 5-2. Pull it downward across your palm and wind it around your wrist.

FIGURE 5-1: Begin all wraps by slipping the loop over your thumb and pulling back toward your wrist.

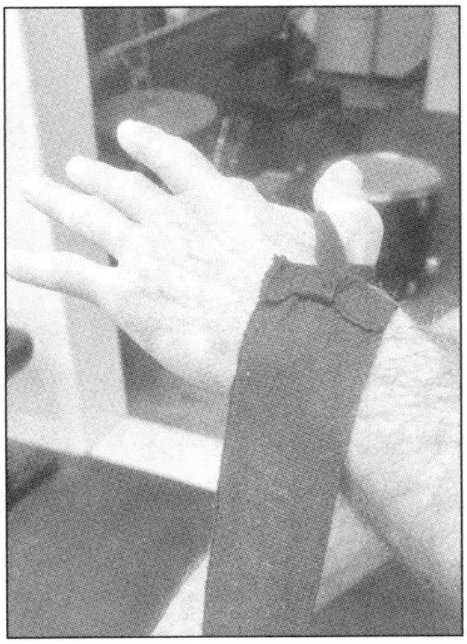

with permission of Cassandra Matthews

FIGURE 5-2: Wind the wrap at least twice around your wrist, firmly but not too tight.

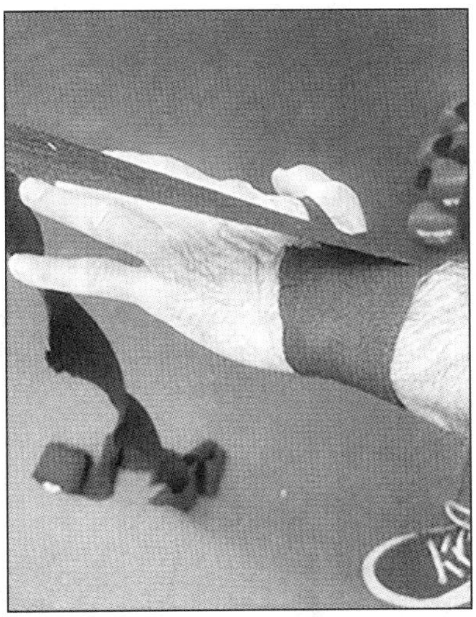

with permission of Cassandra Matthews

Next, pull it between your ring and middle fingers (see Figure 5-3), down across your palm once again, and around your wrist again. Then do the same thing between your middle and index finger and once again go around your wrist. The wrap should be firm between your fingers with no sagging.

Now it's time to wind it across your knuckles. (See Figure 5-4.) I find that four winds is right for my hands, but since hand sizes vary, you may need more or less.

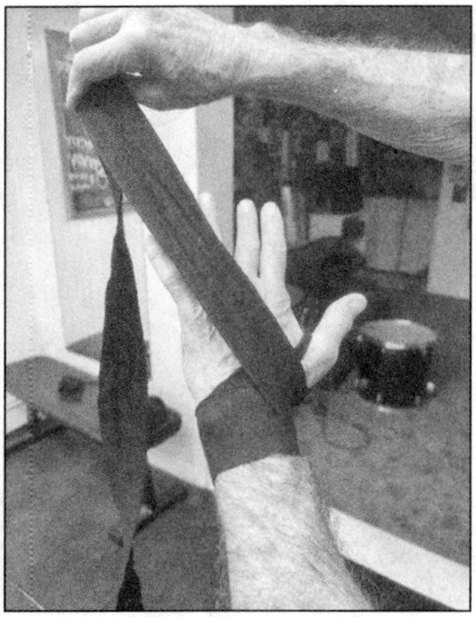

FIGURE 5-3: Pull the wrap between your ring and little fingers and down across your palm.

with permission of Cassandra Matthews

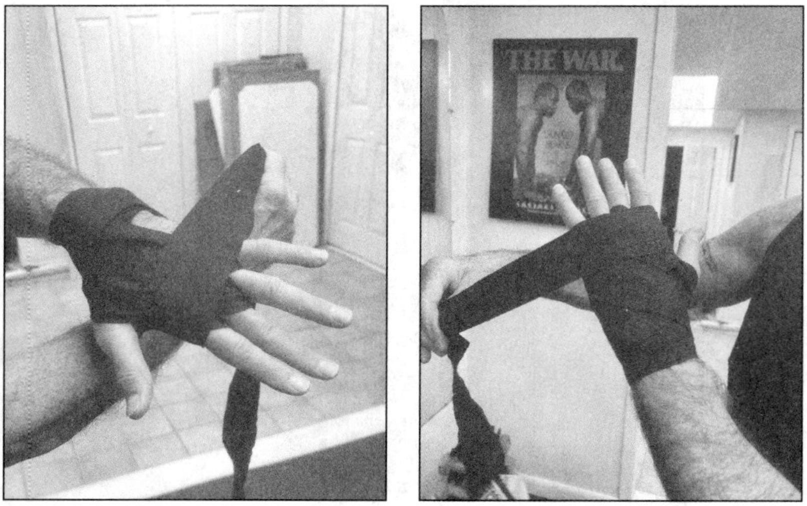

FIGURE 5-4: Wind the wrap around your knuckles four times to keep the metacarpals from spreading on impact.

with permission of Cassandra Matthews

After the four winds, crisscross the wrap across your palm (see Figure 5-6) and wrap it around your wrist. Then wrap it around your knuckles again once or twice more, depending on your hand size and how much wrap you have left. Crisscross the remaining wrap across the back of your hand (see Figure 5-5) and secure the wrap at your wrist with the Velcro.

Squeeze your hand into your glove and bingo! You're ready to punch. (See Figure 5-6.)

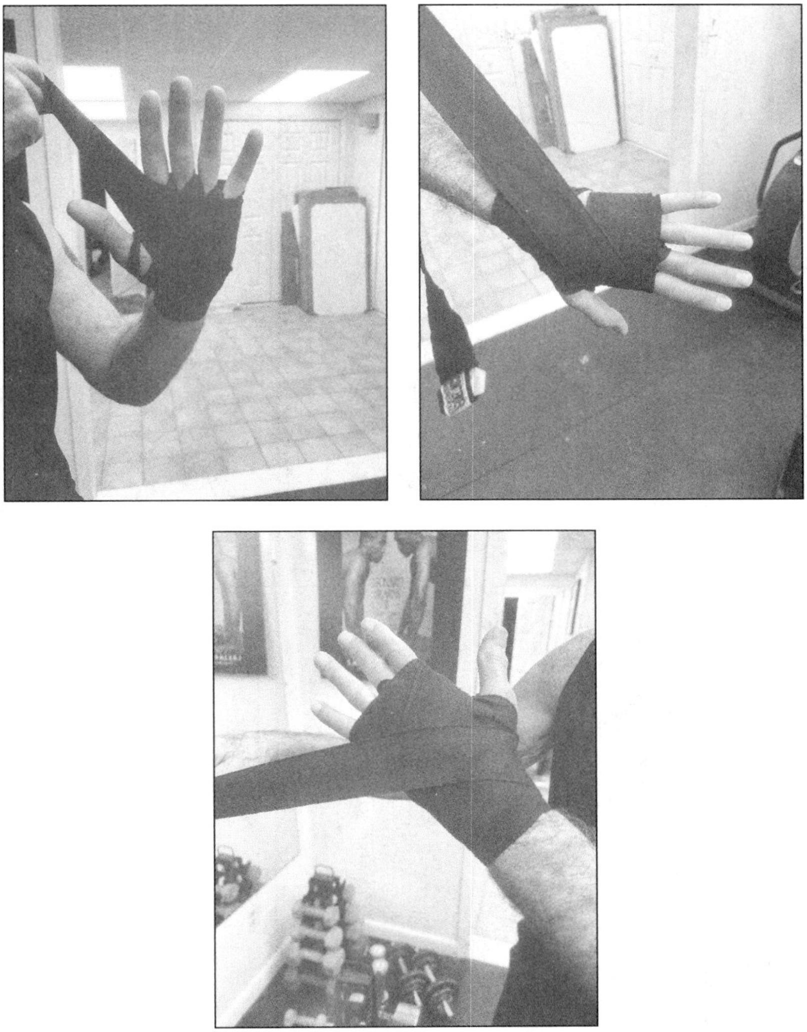

FIGURE 5-5: Crisscross the wrap neatly over the back of your hand.

with permission of Cassandra Matthews

Opting for ready-made wraps

Some of my clients simply refuse to wrap their hands in the traditional fashion and opt for ready-made wraps, which are essentially padded fingerless gloves with a short length of cloth to wrap around the wrist, as shown in Figure 5-7. Obviously, these are easier and more convenient for some people, but I find them unsuitable for an intense bag workout because they provide only knuckle protection and very little wrist support. In fact, I have had several clients injure their wrists using these and they found those injuries disappeared when I wrapped their hands with my method. Use them if you insist, but I don't recommend them.

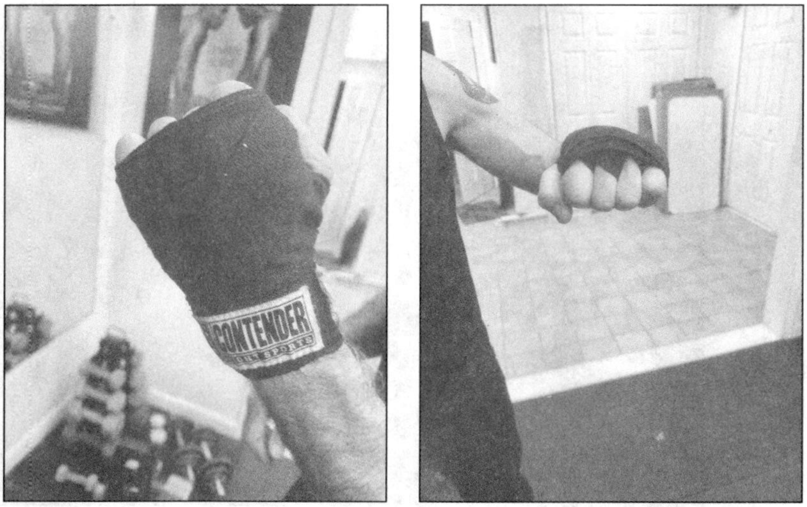

FIGURE 5-6: A well-wrapped fist, ready for action.

with permission of Cassandra Matthews

FIGURE 5-7: A ready-made hand wrap. Slip 'em on and you're ready to go.

Courtesy of TITLE Boxing

Looking at gel knuckle guards

Some boxing manufacturers sell gel-infused pads or O-shaped rings that can be positioned under the hand wraps to provide a little more protection for the knuckles. (See Figure 5-8.) These are effective for beginners or when rehabbing a knuckle injury, but in most cases a good pair of gloves provides all the protection necessary for a heavy bag or hand pad workout.

FIGURE 5-8: If you need a little extra knuckle protection, try these gel knuckle shields.

Courtesy of TITLE Boxing

Fight-night wraps

The wraps you wear on fight night are markedly different from training wraps. For one thing, fight-night wraps are white medical gauze rather than woven cloth. For another, there are specific rules about the length of the wraps and how they're applied. The Nevada State Athletic Commission specifies no more than 15 yards of gauze and 6 feet of adhesive tape per hand, and that the tape cannot be excessive over the knuckles. Also, the wrapping process must be witnessed by a commission inspector as well as a representative of the boxer's opponent to ensure that nothing illegal has been placed under the wraps, which are then initialed by the inspector to prove they have not been tampered with after the inspector leaves the dressing room.

HISTORICAL TIDBIT

There have been at least two well-publicized incidents of glove tampering in major boxing matches. In 1983, it was discovered that padding had been removed from the gloves of welterweight Luis Resto before his fight against Billy Collins Jr. at Madison Square Garden. The "loaded" gloves resulted in severe eye injuries for Collins, who never fought again. Resto and his trainer, Panama Lewis, were convicted of criminal conspiracy, and Resto spent two years in prison.

In 2009, welterweight Antonio Margarito was found to have a plaster-like substance beneath his hand wraps before a bout with Shane Mosley. He was suspended from boxing for a year.

And in the 1950s, Jack Kearns, the former manager of Jack Dempsey, claimed he had loaded his fighter's hands with plaster before his title-winning bout with Jess

Willard in 1919. The accusation was debunked when experiments using Kearns's method failed to duplicate the results he claimed to have achieved.

Protecting That Baby Face

If you are planning to spar, the first area that must be protected is the area above your neck. The best way to do this, of course, is to develop your defense so that you don't get hit very often or very cleanly. This is covered in Chapter 11. But even with the best defense, you need some protection for your head to blunt the impact of potentially damaging blows.

Headguards

Probably the most misunderstood piece of boxing equipment is the headguard, because most people believe wearing one will cushion the impact of blows and protect the boxer from brain injury. This is only true to an extent. A headguard will blunt some of the impact of the punch, but it will not eliminate the concussive effect on the brain. Simply put, the human brain is similar to a handful of Jello floating in fluid inside a hard shell. When hit by a punch, that handful of Jello sloshes back and forth inside the cup, and if hit hard enough it will make contact with that shell (the skull). No headguard ever designed will stop that from happening.

What the headguard is most effective at is preventing a boxer from being cut by an accidental or deliberate clash of heads. When boxers are fighting in close, their heads often bang together. This is known as a butt, and cuts caused by severe butts have often decided the outcome of fights. The reason boxers wear headguards in training is to prevent this from happening during a sparring session, potentially causing a fight to be canceled and money to be lost.

Minimalist

This "old-school" type of headgear worn by boxers such as Jack Dempsey in the 1920s (see Figure 5-9) and Joe Louis in the '40s were barely more than a padded strip of leather across the forehead, designed to protect the boxer from being cut by head butts in sparring. These are nearly impossible to find these days, but a similar model was being worn in training by Mike Tyson as recently as the late '80s, perhaps in tribute to the old fighters Tyson admired. One asset of the old-school headguard was its small size, making it less likely to be hit by grazing punches, an essential feature for boxers who relied on a bobbing and weaving defense.

FIGURE 5-9: Jack Dempsey wearing a 1920s-style minimalist headguard.

Keystone/Getty Images

Helmet type

Most modern headgears are of the "helmet" type, which are heavily padded and include cheek protectors that run down both sides of the face. (See Figure 5-10.) The cheek protection provides more coverage over the face, sometimes narrowing the open area to a slit just wide enough to allow vision. This type of headguard is heavier and larger than the minimalist variety. A well-made genuine leather headguard costs about $100.

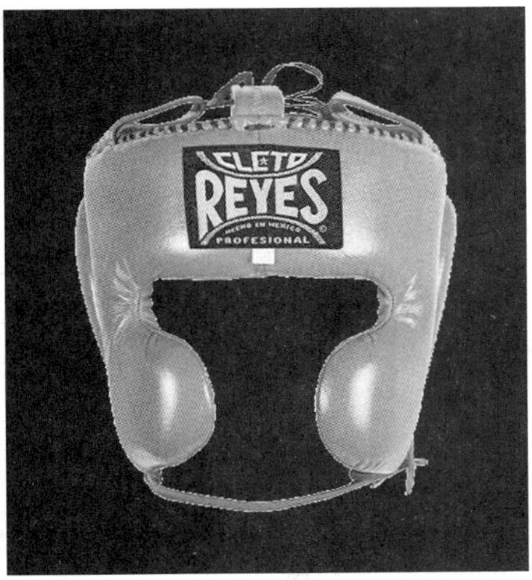

FIGURE 5-10: A typical helmet-type headguard.

Courtesy of CLETO REYES

Full face

Full-face headguards range from the type that has not only cheek protection but a padded leather bar that runs completely across the jaw and chin area, to the type that resembles a baseball catcher's or hockey goalie's mask, with high-impact plastic crossbars that prevent a glove from ever touching the face. (See Figure 5-11.) Some models allow you to remove the bars for a more conventional headguard experience. Expect to pay between $60 and $100 for a full-face headgear.

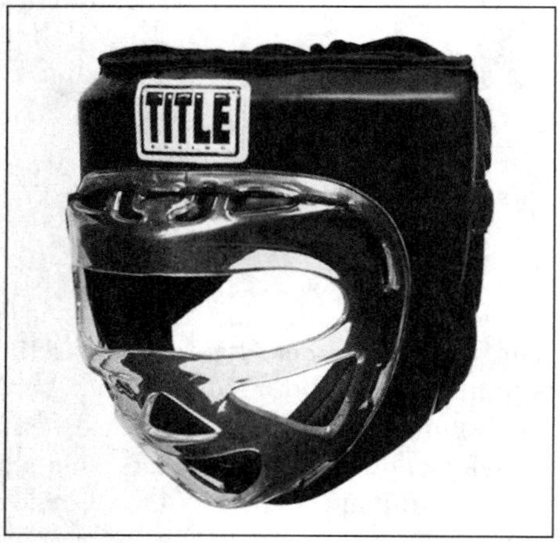

FIGURE 5-11: A full-face, catcher's mask-type headguard.

Courtesy of TITLE Boxing

One more layer of protection

The use of petroleum jellies such as Vaseline is allowed and encouraged on the faces of boxers both in sparring and on fight night. This is to help the punches slide off the face. It is also useful in conditioning the leather of your boxing gloves. It's definitely worth investing in a jar or two.

Keeping the Sensitive Parts Safe and Secure

Of course, the head and midsection are not the only vulnerable areas on a boxer's body. Both male and female boxers wear equipment to protect particularly vulnerable areas of the body which, while illegal to hit in a match, still occasionally get in the way of punches.

Foul-proof cups

There is a reason why punches "below the belt" are illegal in boxing, as any male who has ever been hit there, even accidentally, can tell you. According to boxing legend, a character who called himself Foulproof Taylor invented and patented a groin protector similar to the one used today, and would demonstrate its effectiveness by challenging people to swing a baseball bat into his lower regions while wearing the device.

True or not, the "foul-proof cup" is an essential piece of boxing equipment and must be worn every time a boxer steps into the ring to spar or to fight. It is basically a padded leather belt about four inches wide that goes around a fighter's waist, with a hard plastic or metal cup attached to cover the fighter's genitals. (See Figure 5-12.) This device will protect vulnerable areas from a straight-on shot, but isn't very effective against a punch that comes up from below. Still, it's better than nothing, and for a piece of equipment so vital, foul-proof cups are remarkably inexpensive, ranging from $25 to $50 for a good one.

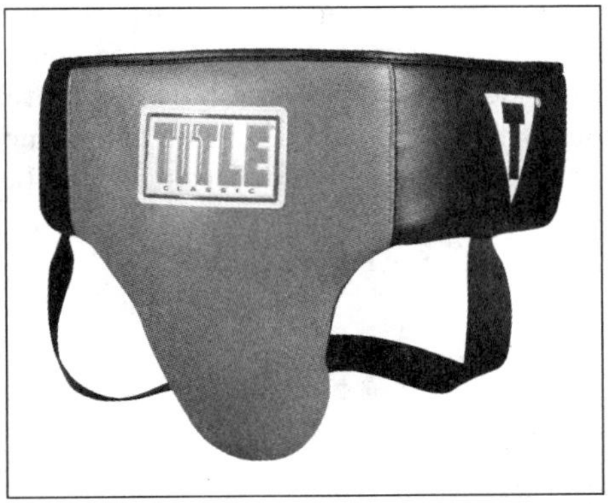

FIGURE 5-12: A standard male foul-proof cup.

Courtesy of TITLE Boxing

Women boxers also wear a cup-type protective device, as shown in Figure 5-13, but it is smaller than those worn by men.

HISTORICAL TIDBIT

The world heavyweight championship changed hands for the first and only time on a foul in 1930 when Max Schmeling went down from a low blow thrown by Jack Sharkey, and Schmeling was declared the winner on a disqualification. In 1996, a non-title heavyweight bout between Riddick Bowe and Andrew Golota touched off a riot inside Madison Square Garden when Golota was disqualified for repeated low blows.

FIGURE 5-13: A smaller foul-proof cup designed for female boxers.

Courtesy of TITLE Boxing

Chest protectors

In addition to groin protection, women boxers are required to wear chest protection in their bouts. Female groin protection differs from the male version in that it is smaller, but still padded to prevent injury to a vulnerable area. (Refer to Figure 5-13.) And although it is an unwritten rule that women boxers will not intentionally hit each other in the breast area, accidents do happen. To prevent injury, female boxers wear modified sports bras with high-impact plastic inserts similar to the cups worn by men. (See Figure 5-14.)

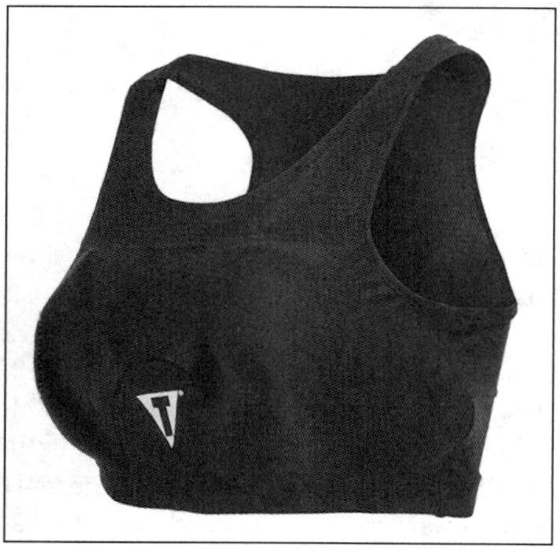

FIGURE 5-14: A chest protector of the type worn by female boxers.

Courtesy of TITLE Boxing

Maintaining That Dazzling Smile

The least expensive piece of boxing safety equipment is also one of the most important. Not only does the mouthpiece protect the teeth, but when properly fitted it creates a tight suction that sets the jaw and makes it less vulnerable to injury. I can attest to the importance of this piece of equipment through personal experience: While sparring with an ill-fitting mouthpiece that came loose in my mouth, I was hit by a left hook that broke my jaw.

Surprisingly, a good boxing mouthpiece can be had for $10 or less. Most are made of a rubber or plastic substance that is briefly plunged into a pot of boiling water to soften it, and then placed over the upper teeth while still warm. Biting down hard on the softened material creates an impression of the teeth, and sucking in provides a solid seal to the mouth and jaw, making it more resistant to punches.

There are more expensive options, too, which are usually fitted by a dentist or oral surgeon, which can run you hundreds of dollars. But for most purposes, a properly fitted "boil-and-bite" mouthpiece will work fine. (See Figure 5-15.)

FIGURE 5-15: A standard "boil-and-bite" mouthguard.

Courtesy of TITLE Boxing

IN THIS CHAPTER

» The equipment you need, and how to use it

» The difference between the speed, heavy, double-end, and cobra bags

» How to get the most out of a hand pad workout

Chapter 6
The Boxer's Basic Toolbox

Although there have been tremendous technological and philosophical advances in fitness training over the past century, the mainstays of boxing training have remained remarkably constant. The bedrocks of a boxing regimen have always been the jump rope, the speed bag, the heavy bag, and the mirror. If those are all you have access to, you have everything you need for an intense and effective boxing workout.

In addition, there are a few other pieces of equipment that can enhance your workout if you have the room and the budget to include them, but they're not absolutely necessary. Let's start with the basics first.

Working the Ropes

Although it has only recently been recognized as a great overall conditioner and incorporated into many modern workout routines, rope skipping has been a key part of boxing training for nearly as long as there has been boxing. A rope-skipping workout can serve as a warmup, or as an intense cardiovascular exercise that increases a boxer's wind and cuts their weight. It improves footwork, makes a boxer light on their feet, and gives a boxer's legs their characteristic bounce. Plus, it's very impressive to watch. The great former welterweight and middleweight champion Sugar Ray Robinson was especially adept at rope skipping and his routine was a highlight for observers of his workouts.

Jump ropes come in many varieties, from the old-school leather type (see Figure 6-1a) to today's "speed ropes" made of thin PVC plastic (see Figure 6-1b) and those with weighted handles (see Figure 6-1c) to provide a more challenging workout. Personally, I find a braided rope covered with plastic segments (see Figure 6-1d) works just fine and provides a strenuous workout. Whichever type you choose, be sure to get one with ball-bearing handles so the rope turns smoothly and effortlessly.

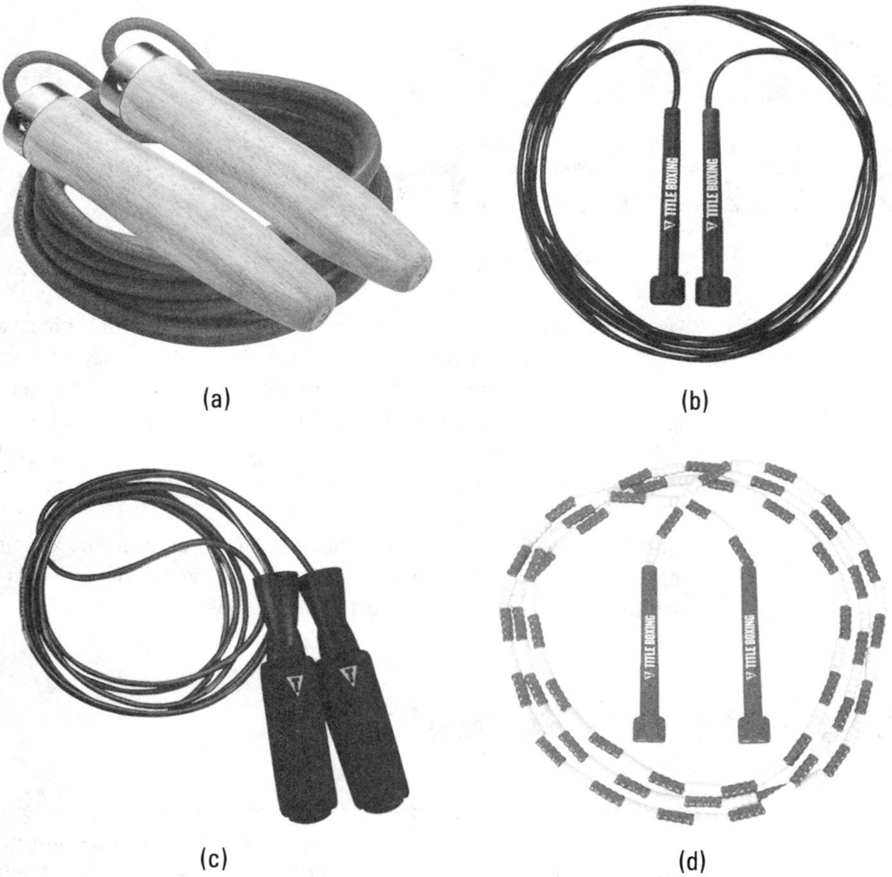

FIGURE 6-1: Four types of jump ropes: (a) old-school leather, (b) speed, (c) weighted handle, and (d) plastic segmented.

Courtesy of TITLE Boxing

Most jump ropes are nine feet long and you must know how to adjust the length correctly or jumping will be extremely difficult. Many modern ropes come with the ability to adjust the length by pulling the rope through the handles and cutting off the excess. But if it's a shared rope or the property of the gym you're training at, there's another approach. The way I determine the correct length is to take both handles together in one hand and step with one foot in the loop at the bottom. I then pull the rope up to my armpit. The ends of the handles should reach precisely to my underarm. If it's higher than that, I tie a knot or two near the handles until the length is exactly right.

Basic rope jumping

The key to effective and enjoyable rope skipping is to stay loose. By this I mean don't jump too high, don't turn the rope too fast, and don't overuse your wrists. Rope skipping done well involves just a slight jump off the ground — remember, the rope is barely a quarter-inch thick, so you only need to come off the ground no more than an inch — a steady, relaxed tempo, and only the slightest movement of your wrists. The ball-bearing handles do most of the work of turning the rope.

If you've never jumped before, it's best to start by jumping with both feet at once, turning the rope lightly and landing on the balls of your feet, as shown in Figure 6-2. Start with the rope behind your back and swing it forward over your head. Don't worry about speed at this point. Your object is consistency, being able to jump without stepping on the rope for extended periods of time. And that takes practice and repetition. But take my word for it, once you figure it out, you never forget it, much like riding a bicycle.

Rope skipping can be strenuous, so start out aiming to go for 30 seconds without stopping. Don't be discouraged if you step on the rope or trip on it. We all do it. Just pick up where you left off. Try to get the timing of the tempo — as the rope hits the floor in front of you, jump up slightly and let it pass under your feet. As you do it, you'll fall into the rhythm of the rope and the speed with which it comes around again. Before you know it, you'll feel emboldened enough to separate those feet.

Advanced skipping techniques

Once you've mastered two-foot jumping, you can begin to branch out a bit. The easiest way to separate those feet at first is to take a modified running step while the rope passes under your feet, as shown in Figure 6-3.

FIGURE 6-2: If you're a beginner, start by jumping with both feet at a time.

with permission of Anthony Policano

FIGURE 6-3: A modified running step is the easiest way to start skipping one foot at a time.

with permission of Anthony Policano

Eventually, you'll learn to bounce on alternate feet, and from there it's a short hop (pun intended) to a heel-and-toe skip where you alternate landing on the heels and toes of your foot, as shown in Figure 6-4. It's not as difficult as it sounds!

FIGURE 6-4: With a little practice you'll soon be doing a heel-and-toe skip that will make you light on your feet in the ring.

with permission of Anthony Policano

Next you want to try crisscrossing the rope without missing a skip. The key here is to cross your arms quickly as the rope comes over your head, and back again as it passes under your feet. It's important that you don't hesitate on the crisscross, because if you do you'll land on the rope. With practice you'll be surprised at how smoothly this works. (And how great it looks to gym-watchers!)

I often start by skipping on both feet, then switch to two skips on each foot, and then to alternating feet on each skip. Later on, I change the step to a heel-and-toe skip, and often finish up with a fast, running type skip for the final 30 seconds. Again, like all boxing techniques, it takes practice and repetition to get it right.

And if you find that you're getting frustrated with the whole thing, there's always this technique, which looks great but is extremely easy: Simply hold both handles in one hand and turn the rope alongside your body while bouncing lightly on your feet. Do that for three minutes and you'll very closely approximate a proper rope-skipping workout.

Power Punching? It's All in the Bags

Hitting the bags is the backbone of every boxing workout, and the one sure way to hone your skill set. The most important are the speed bag and the heavy bag, but there's also a range of specialty bags, which are variations on those two, each of which provide a different type of workout and help fine-tune a different set of skills.

Getting up to speed with the speed bag

So what exactly is a speed bag? (See Figure 6-5.)

It's a teardrop-shaped leather bag with welted seams that hangs from a swivel mounted to a circular platform, usually made of thick wood. The platform is generally mounted to a wall to reduce vibrations, but there are also speed bag platforms that hang from the same type of steel rack that supports heavy bags (more on that later in this chapter). The platform usually has a cranking mechanism to adjust its height, and a professional-quality swivel has ball bearings to allow the bag not only to move forward and backward but also to spin on its axis, making it all the more difficult to hit solidly. A good-quality leather speed bag runs between $50 and $100. A serviceable platform can be had for about $150, but the best cost upward of $500. Swivels generally cost between $25 and $50, and many screw into a flange mounted on the platform, making it easier to switch out bags. Many boxers like to bring their own speed bags to the gym, already mounted on a swivel, and screw them into the flange on the gym's platform. (See Figure 6-6.)

FIGURE 6-5: Speed bags come in various sizes from peanut-sized (5" x 8") to large (10" x 12").

Courtesy of the author

FIGURE 6-6: A professional speed bag setup with bag, platform, and swivel.

Courtesy of the author

Few sounds are more characteristic of a boxing gym than the rhythmic rat-tat-tat of a speed bag, and few gym experiences are more satisfying than mastering this basic piece of boxing equipment. A few rounds on speed bag at the start of your workout is a great warmup for the more intense exercises to follow. It's also excellent at building muscle endurance and stamina; you'll be surprised at how difficult it is at first to keep your hands up for a full three minutes, which is essential for an effective speed bag workout. Plus, it looks and sounds very impressive to make that little bag sing out its distinctive drumbeat. These days, speed bag punching is not only for boxers; I've seen speed bag platforms in the clubhouse of professional baseball and hockey teams, two sports that rely heavily on hand-eye coordination.

But how do you progress from your crude initial attempts at trying to hit the bag even twice in a row to that beautiful, seamless pulsation of a bag well-struck? As in most pursuits involving coordination and rhythm, speed — or more accurately, the lack thereof — is key.

Starting out big and slow

All speed bags have the same basic teardrop shape, with one significant difference. They come in several sizes, ranging from large (approximately 7 × 10 inches) to extra small (approximately 4 × 7 inches) (refer to Figure 6-5). Obviously, the smaller the bag, the faster the rebound, the higher the degree of difficulty, and the steeper the learning curve. Of course, the reverse is true as well. That's why speed bag novices are well advised to start out with the largest bag available, such as the bag shown in Figure 6-7. The bigger target and slower rebound are much easier for newbies to deal with and facilitate your learning the tempo and rhythm of good speed bag hitting. And believe it or not, when you master the smallest speed bags, known as "peanut" bags, you'll find it difficult to go back to hitting that big blunderbuss you started out with.

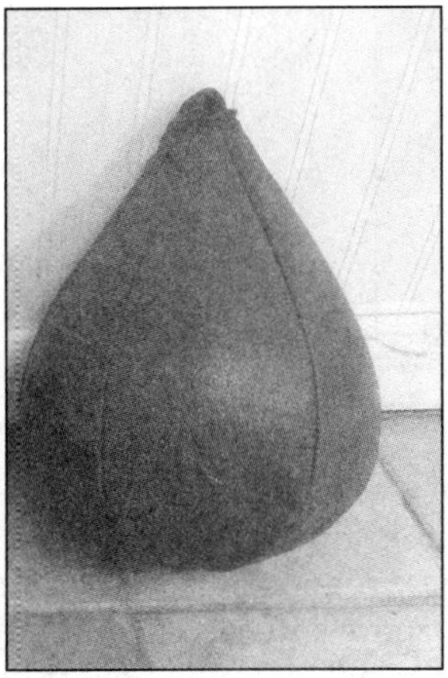

FIGURE 6-7: A large speed bag is easier to start out with.

Courtesy of the author

Mastering the tempo

First off, you should wrap your hands before hitting the speed bag, but gloves are not necessary. In fact, I find that using any sort of gloves on the speed bag makes the workout more difficult. But if you like, you can wear a pair of thin gloves without much padding on the knuckles. It's important to "feel" the bag as you hit it, and wearing gloves only makes that more difficult.

Also important is dialing in the proper height of the bag. The bottom of the bag should be at the level of your chin, with the widest part of the bag just about at eye level. If you have an adjustable speed bag platform, this is easy to do. If not, most gyms have small wooden platforms of varying heights for boxers needing more height to stand on.

When you've achieved the proper height, take your normal boxing stance (see Figure 6-8) close enough to the bag so you're not reaching for it.

FIGURE 6-8: Take your normal boxing stance in front of the speed bag.

with permission of Anthony Policano

Begin hitting it with the side of your front hand (see Figure 6-9), just one hand at a time, and not too hard. You need to get into the rhythm of hitting the bag on every third bounce. In other words, after you strike the bag, it will bounce off the platform moving away from you, bounce off the platform again on its return, and once more moving away from you before you hit it again. There is a distinctive 1-2-3, 1-2-3, 1-2-3 cadence to it — musicians refer to this rhythm as "triplets" — and once you figure out this timing, you'll have taken a big step toward speed bag mastery.

When you get comfortable hitting the bag with just your front hand, you can begin alternating your hands in a rolling motion, front hand, back hand, 1-2-3, 1-2-3. This takes time, concentration, and endurance, because your natural inclination will be to let your hands drop. If you do that, you'll never get them back up in time to hit the bag again in the right tempo. Continue practicing striking the bag with alternate hands before trying to get fancy.

FIGURE 6-9: Start by hitting the bag with the side of your front hand.

with permission of Anthony Policano

Advanced techniques

Once you've gotten the alternate hands technique down pat, you can experiment with more advanced forms of speed bag hitting. My favorite is to hit it twice with each hand, first striking it with the side of my front hand (refer to Figure 6-9) followed by a straight shot from my rear hand, then hitting it with the side of my rear hand to straighten it out for a straight shot from my front hand (see Figure 6-10). I repeat the sequence for the remainder of the round. It's not as complicated as it sounds! The thinking behind this is that every other punch will be delivered in the manner of a punch in a real fight, with the backhand or side-hand punch (neither of which are ever thrown in the ring) being used only to correct the bag's course for the next shot.

An even more advanced technique is to hit the bag with combinations, for example a one-two or a hook, cross, and hook. This is easiest to do on a large speed bag, but still very difficult and usually only done by professionals with years of experience. Others like to occasionally hit the bag with their elbows, but since this has little use in a fight or sparring session — in fact, it will get you disqualified — I fail to see the value in it except for the purpose of amusing any onlookers.

The same goes for the technique of hitting the bag by rolling your hands without allowing the bag to strike the platform on the rebound, as shown in Figure 6-11. In this technique, the bag only hits the platform in front of you once and is immediately hit again. This might serve as an occasional endurance exercise — try keeping that going for a full three minutes! — but like the elbow technique, this looks a lot more impressive than it is useful.

FIGURE 6-10: Next, hit the bag with a straight punch with your rear hand as it comes back to you. Then hit it with the side of your rear hand to set it up for a straight punch with your front hand, and so on.

with permission of Anthony Policano

FIGURES 6-11: The "rolling fists" technique for hitting the speed bag.

with permission of Anthony Policano

Going smaller — and faster

If you're diligent about learning the speed bag, you'll inevitably choose smaller and faster bags as your skills improve. The techniques are the same, but hitting a small or peanut bag requires greater concentration and hand-eye coordination. Eventually, you'll progress to the point that you can do a solid three minutes on a peanut-sized bag, which will really impress your friends!

Going Heavy with the Heavy Bag

The heavy bag is probably the oldest and most widely used piece of boxing equipment. Going back to the 19th century, you come across accounts of great fighters such as John L. Sullivan and Jack Dempsey hitting makeshift heavy bags as boys, and former heavyweight champion Joe Frazier has talked about hitting a canvas sack filled with detritus such as rags, corn cobs, and even brick fragments that he hung from the branch of an oak tree in his family's backyard in Beaufort, South Carolina, when he was a preteen. To this day, the heavy bag remains a mainstay of any boxing workout, as indispensable as a bat in a baseball game.

The heavy bag is exactly what it sounds like: a long, cylindrical object generally about 12 inches in diameter, weighing between 75 and 200 pounds or more (see Figure 6-12). Its exterior can be made of leather, synthetic leather, or canvas and it's filled so that it's solid but somewhat forgiving on impact. The traditional filling for a heavy bag was tightly packed shredded fabric scraps, but modern heavy bags now incorporate foam rubber or gel liners to increase shock absorption and mitigate injury. Water-filled heavy bags (see Figure 6-13) are also popular nowadays because they're significantly softer to hit while still carrying plenty of weight. They also provide a satisfying *crack!* sound when struck properly, which I've found to be a great motivator in my classes.

Heavy bags are generally hung from the ceiling of a gym by chains and a swivel attached to a carabiner. This allows the bag not only to swing back and forth, but also to rotate on its axis, which are signs that the bag is not being hit correctly (more on this below). Some gyms include a spring between the chains and the swivel to provide some up and down movement of the bag as well.

For those who are unable to hang a bag from the ceiling, there are a variety of free-standing heavy bags on the market that sit on a base, usually filled with water or sand, allowing them to be used virtually anywhere (see Figure 6-14).

FIGURE 6-12: A standard heavy bag, one of the oldest and most useful pieces of boxing equipment.

Courtesy of TITLE Boxing

FIGURE 6-13: A water-filled heavy bag is easier on the knuckles and shoulders.

Courtesy of TITLE Boxing

Whichever bag you choose, it's important to wrap your hands properly before hitting a heavy bag and to wear a well-padded pair of specially constructed bag gloves of between 12 and 16 ounces to protect your hands and wrists from the repetitive pounding of a good heavy bag workout.

FIGURE 6-14: A free-standing heavy bag is great if you have nowhere to hang a traditional bag.

Courtesy of TITLE Boxing

The proper way to hit a heavy bag

The first thing we must know about the heavy bag is that its primary use is to develop punching power. Hitting the heavy bag correctly develops your shoulders, your hips, and your core. It also ingrains in your brain and muscles the proper mechanics of delivering a powerful punch. Although you'll eventually throw combinations on this bag, its main purpose is to condition you to hit hard with every punch.

When hitting the heavy bag, you should take your normal fighting stance — hands up, feet slightly more than shoulder-width apart, profiled to the bag with your dominant hand in back (see Figure 6-15). Adjust your distance so that your punch lands with maximum power and snap. If you're too far away from the bag, your punches will land thinly and you'll put yourself at risk of hyperextending your elbow. If you're too close, you'll smother your punches, robbing them of much of their power. Gauging your distance, both against the bag and against an opponent, is an essential skill that you must master.

Start out by just practicing your jab. Take a half step forward with your front foot and snap your front hand, palm down, into the bag. Return immediately to your starting position and do it again. And again. And again, until it feels comfortable and natural.

Next, practice throwing only your dominant, or back, hand. Do not switch your foot position; learn to pivot your rear hip and the toes of your back foot to transfer the weight of your body through your fist. Again, return immediately to your starting position, and repeat as many times as necessary to feel comfortable with the movement.

FIGURE 6-15: Take your normal stance when hitting the heavy bag and find the right distance to land with maximum power.

Courtesy of TITLE Boxing

Now, it's time to add the one-two, your jab followed immediately by your cross, and then reset yourself into your basic stance. The important thing to remember is to snap the bag, not push it. You'll know you're doing it right if the bag remains stationary — or close to it — while imparting that good cracking sound on impact. If the bag swings or moves side to side, you're pushing it. Understand the difference.

Once you've mastered the basics of snapping your straight punches into the bag, you can move on to hooks and uppercuts and an almost endless assortment of combinations. The proper delivery of those punches is covered in Chapters 8 and 9.

Time for reflection

Believe it or not, your best friend in the gym will not be your trainer. It will be the mirror that should be on the wall of every boxing gym. In fact, the best boxing gyms have mirrors on all four walls. Why?

Because checking your reflection as you shadowbox or hit the bags is the only real way to see your form and what bad habits you're falling into, if any (see Figure 6-16). Specifically, the mirror lets you know if you're dropping your hands, if your feet are too far apart, if you're remembering to step forward with your jab and rotating your hips with your cross, if you're turning your fists over on impact, if you're pulling your fists back into your starting position after a combination, and so on.

These things are hard to be aware of in the middle of an intense workout, but an occasional glance in the mirror, much like you periodically scan your dashboard while driving, will remind you of what you're doing wrong. And seeing your mistakes for yourself is a lot more effective than hearing about them from an observer.

FIGURE 6-16: Your mirror will show you mistakes you had no idea you were making. Don't be afraid to use it.

with permission of Anthony Policano

Specialty Bags

Several types of bags provide a different kind of workout than you get on a conventional speed or heavy bag and are worth considering adding to your routine.

Uppercut bags

The uppercut bag is simply a standard heavy bag, cylindrical in shape, that hangs horizontally rather than vertically, as shown in Figure 6-17. This makes it easier to hit with uppercuts, which tend to slide off the surface of a conventional heavy bag. The uppercut bag is generally mounted at about a boxer's chin level, providing an ample hitting surface for punches that come up from underneath rather than straight from the shoulder.

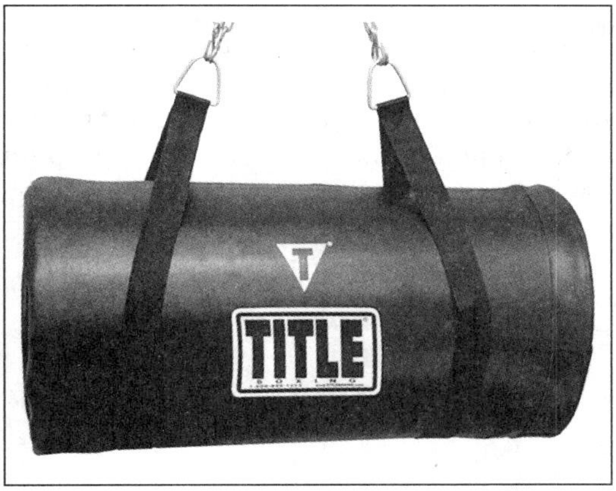

FIGURE 6-17: This horizontally hanging heavy bag is designed specifically to practice uppercuts.

Courtesy of TITLE Boxing

Torso bags

A very popular form of heavy bag is the torso bag, which is basically the upper torso of a man made of durable rubber filled with a fibrous material that simulates the feel of the impact of a punch upon the human body (see Figure 6-18). Torso bags are usually free-standing, on a broad plastic base that can be filled with water to provide heft and stability. Torso bags are expensive; they generally run between $300 and $400.

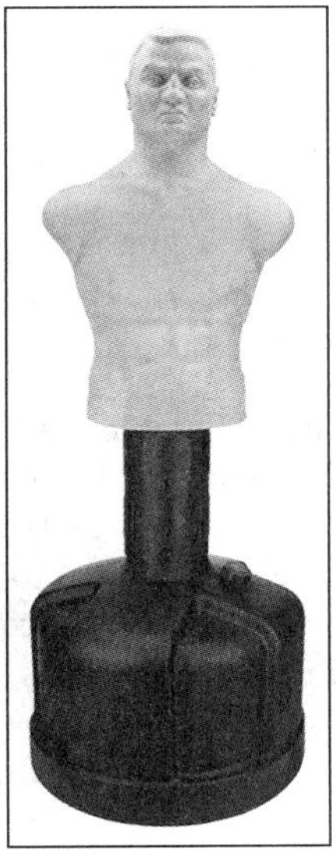

FIGURE 6-18: A torso bag is easy on the hands and allows you to practice hitting specific vulnerable areas of the body.

with permission of Anthony Policano

Aside from the realistic feel of the punches, a torso bag allows a boxer to accurately target vulnerable areas of the body. Because of its lifelike design, the torso bag allows the boxer to fine-tune punches to the solar plexus (see Figure 6-19), ribs (see Figure 6-20), chin, and jaw, which can only be approximated on a conventional heavy bag. And the rubber surface is a lot more forgiving on the wrists and knuckles.

FIGURE 6-19: The torso bag is great for honing your solar plexus punch.

with permission of Anthony Policano

Doing the double-end bag rag

Like the speed bag, the double-end bag is an inflatable leather bag, but rather than being teardrop-shaped and attached to a swivel, it is round and attached to the floor and ceiling by bungee-type cords (see Figure 6-21). Double-end bags range from about the size of a basketball (the easiest to hit) to about the size of a baseball (very difficult and recommended only for highly experienced boxers). The bag should hang at about eye level, and the bungee cords should be adjusted to match your skill level. Too tight and the bag will move too quickly to be hit by more than one punch at a time. Too loose and the action of the bag will be dead. It takes time and patience to find the sweet spot.

FIGURE 6-20: The torso bag also provides an excellent target for your hook to the ribs.

with permission of Anthony Policano

FIGURE 6-21: Ready to level up your hand-eye coordination? Use the double-end bag.

Courtesy of TITLE Boxing

Double-end bags need some room to swing, so if you have a small workout space it may be problematic to install one. Also, the bag must be anchored both at the ceiling (via an S-hook or carabiner) and at the floor (either by being weighted down with sandbags or bolted into the ground). You can get away with wearing just hand wraps when hitting the double-end bag, but make sure to tape over the S-hooks that connect the bungee cords at the top and bottom of the bag to avoid being cut by them.

A double-end bag workout combines some of the attributes of both the speed and heavy bags; you can hit it as hard as you like, but you need quick reflexes and good hand-eye coordination to hit it consistently with combinations (see Figure 6-22). An added feature of the double-end bag is that if you aren't paying close attention, it can whack you upside the head as it comes back. So not only is it a useful tool to develop your offense — the bag's tendency to move side to side or rotate forces you to punch short and straight — it also reminds you to keep your eyes open and move your head from side to side to avoid punches.

FIGURE 6-22: You can hit the double-end bag hard, but be careful it doesn't hit you back!

with permission of Anthony Policano

Similar to learning to hit the speed bag, you should start slowly on the double-end bag. Take your normal fighting stance (see Figure 6-23) and practice hitting it only with your jab. Let it go and then hit it again as it comes back to you. Of course, the harder you hit it, the faster it comes back, so in the beginning it's best not to hit it with your best shot.

Learn to control it with your jab, constantly moving to adjust your angle, and when you have that down, try your one-two combo on it. Eventually, you'll be able to add a hook to the mix, but it must be a short, tight hook, not a wide, looping swing, as shown in Figure 6-24. The double-end will be frustrating at first, but stay with it. You'll find it well worth the trouble.

FIGURE 6-23: Take your normal fighting stance in front of the double-end bag.

with permission of Anthony Policano

FIGURE 6-24: A double-end bag provides a combination speed and power workout. Keep your hook short and tight!

with permission of Anthony Policano

Crushing it with the cobra bag

The cobra bag is a variation of the double-end bag, only instead of being anchored to the ceiling, the bag sits atop a pole and a heavy-duty steel spring, which provides its action, as shown in Figure 6-25. Some cobra bags have an inflatable leather ball as the striking surface, others a ball made of extra-firm foam rubber. Like the double-end bag, the cobra's platform must either be weighted down with sand bags or bolted to the floor. And like the double-end bag, the cobra can come back to bite you if you're not vigilant about your defense.

FIGURE 6-25: The cobra bag is similar to the double-end bag, but a little slower and a lot firmer. Be careful!

Courtesy of TITLE Boxing

Because the steel spring is more stable than a bungee cord, the cobra's movement is a bit slower and more consistent than the double-end, and a bit easier to hit accurately. (See Figure 6-26.) And if you choose one with a solid foam ball, it's a little bit harder on the hands than the double-end. You should always wrap and wear the same gloves you use on the heavy bag when hitting the cobra bag.

Because it's slightly slower than the double-end bag, you should be able to hit it with one-twos right away. Make sure you provide plenty of room to move freely around the cobra bag. As in a double-end workout, you'll find yourself constantly readjusting your angle of attack to coincide with the bag's movement.

FIGURE 6-26: Hit the cobra bag as hard as you can but again, keep your punches short and sweet.

with permission of Anthony Policano

Getting a Handle on Hand Pads

Hand pads are exactly what the name implies, a pair of padded or air-filled mitts, either flat or slightly curved, worn over the hands of a coach who acts as a de facto sparring partner (see Figure 6-27). In fact, a good hand pad workout is the closest you can come to sparring, only without getting hit. A skillful coach will throw mock punches at you to work on your ducking, slipping, bobbing, weaving, and counterpunching.

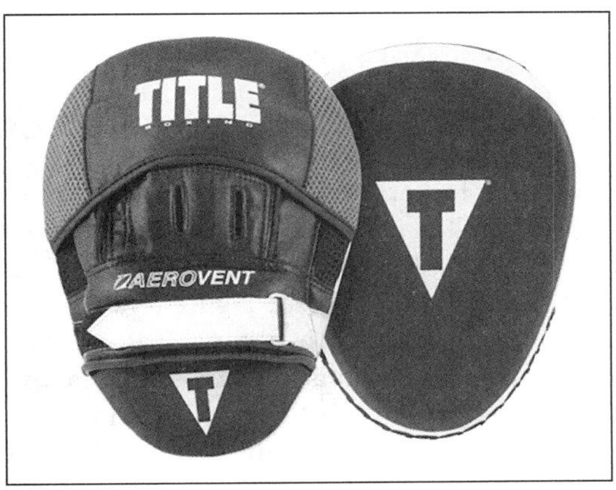

FIGURE 6-27: A typical pair of hand pads.

Courtesy of TITLE Boxing

Hitting hand pads correctly

As in the other workouts above, you should take your normal fighting stance when hitting hand pads and execute your punches as if you were hitting an opponent, as shown in Figure 6-28. You should punch not *at* the pads, but *through* them, with full force, and after each combination, you should reset — that is, return to your fighting stance — before launching the next combo. Listen carefully to your coach or trainer, who will shout which punches or combinations to throw next, and keep your eyes open for the counterpunch!

FIGURE 6-28: In a hand pad drill, take your normal fighting stance and punch *through* the mitts, not *at* them.

with permission of Anthony Policano

Catching hand pads correctly

A hand pad drill is the best opportunity for a coach to observe a client's form and correct mistakes. From the coach's vantage point, it's easy to see if the boxer's stance is too square, if their feet are in the proper position, and if they're dropping their hands. A good coach will make a hand pad drill into a mock sparring session, moving around the ring or gym floor, changing the position of the targets, throwing mock punches to practice slipping (see Figure 6-29), and calling out a wide variety of combinations over the course of a round. I also like to occasionally meet my boxer's punch with the pad — that is, move the pad into the punch — because it provides a resounding impact that is both encouraging and motivating. I also like to move the pad away from the boxer if they have a tendency not to follow through or fully extend the punch. We often play a game in which I move around the ring with my pads down, and then quickly raise them, shouting "Now!" That teaches the boxer not to commit themselves too soon and to be ready to react instantaneously when they see the target.

FIGURE 6-29: Working on a slip-and-counter drill with the pads.

with permission of Anthony Policano

Adding useful pad drills to your training regimen

With beginner boxers I often use a drill that emphasizes technique and repetition, performed in a three-minute round in 30-second chunks. For example, for the first 30 seconds I have them throw only one-twos. For the next 30 seconds, they add a hook, and for the next 30 seconds they throw perhaps a one-two-hook and cross. Other days, we work on body punches or uppercuts or a slip-and-counter drill. It's up to the coach/trainer to keep the hand pad drill both vigorous enough to condition the fighter and varied enough to maintain their interest. I describe several hand pad drills in more detail in Chapter 12.

Boxing with a Reflex Ball

A great little drill to add to your workout is to get a boxing reflex ball, which is simply a soft rubber ball at the end of an elastic thread attached to a band you wear around your head (see Figure 6-30).

It's similar to the wooden paddle with a small rubber ball toy that was popular some years back, but this one actually serves a purpose. It makes a fine warmup, and mastering it — which takes a little practice — improves your hand-eye coordination and your reaction times. Plus, because the elastic thread is so thin, from a distance it looks like you're performing some kind of magical Jedi mind trick. (See Figure 6-31.) As with the speed bag, start with the bigger, slower ball and work your way up. After a few hours of practice you'll be hitting it with hooks, jabs, and crosses. You can find reflex balls online for as little as $10.

FIGURE 6-30: The boxing reflex ball looks like a kid's toy, but it's not so easy to master!

Courtesy of TITLE Boxing

FIGURE 6-31: Batting around the reflex ball as a warmup.

with permission of Anthony Policano

3

Let's Start Punching

IN THIS PART . . .

Learn the most basic of boxing techniques, the fighting stance.

Understand how hip rotation and weight transference equals punching power.

Master the mechanics of the jab, an essential setup tool for all boxers.

Practice the footwork needed for an effective jab.

Learn the "ol' one-two," boxing's most basic combination.

IN THIS CHAPTER

» Developing a proper stance

» Maintaining your balance in the ring

» Learning to punch like a pro

» Mastering the art of weight transfer and hip rotation

Chapter 7

Mastering the Basics

Whether you're a dancer à la Muhammad Ali or a come-forward brawler like Joe Frazier, the basic starting point for all boxers is the same: the stance. In many ways, boxing is improvisation, but all forms of improv begin with a basic premise. In boxing, that premise is your fighting stance. Your stance is your foundation and your starting point. It is the basis from which all the rest comes: your offense, defense, and mobility. It is the home base to which you will always return after throwing a combination, being hit with a punch, breaking from a clinch, or simply stepping back to take a breather. Before we go any deeper into the mechanics of punching and avoiding punches, it is important to understand the basic fighting stance.

Developing a Fighting Stance

Whether you're right-handed or left-handed, the basic boxing stance is the same: feet slightly more than shoulder-width apart, knees slightly bent, hands up around cheekbone level with palms facing one another, elbows tight to the body, chin tucked down into your chest, and eyes up on your opponent. (See Figure 7-1.) Although "Peek-a-boo" type fighters like Floyd Patterson and Mike Tyson often stood square to their opponents, I believe it is better — that is, safer — to stand profiled to your opponent, giving as little access to your body as possible. That means your front hand (left if you're a righty, right if you're a lefty) will be about six inches closer to your opponent than your back, or power hand. We will make up for that discrepancy of distance later when we discuss the hip rotation while throwing a punch.

FIGURE 7-1: Front and side view of the basic boxing stance: feet shoulder-width apart, knees slightly bent, hands up, and chin down.

with permission of Anthony Policano

REMEMBER

Hands up, chin down is your mantra. Repeat as necessary throughout your workout.

Working on balance and mobility

It's imperative that no matter where you move in the ring — forward, backward, or side-to-side — you maintain the correct distance between your feet, which, as mentioned above, is slightly wider than shoulder width. You must be careful not to allow your feet to cross, come together, or get too far apart. All these will compromise your balance, leaving you vulnerable to getting hit and robbing significant power from your punches. Some boxing equipment manufacturers sell a device — a resistance band that attaches to both ankles — to teach a boxer to maintain the proper leg spacing, but this is not necessary. Just remember that when your front foot advances, the back foot follows it the same distance, and when your rear foot retreats, the front foot must also do so.

Another thing to remember is that as your opponent moves, you must move with them while maintaining your stance and balance. This is done by pivoting on your front foot in the direction your opponent is moving and following with your rear foot at the proper distance. I use an agility ladder (see Figure 7-2) with my clients to work on this aspect of the sport, having them step into each box with their front foot while throwing a jab, then stepping back out and sliding to the next one. When they reach the end of the ladder, they quickly pivot around and repeat the drill in the opposite direction. (See Figure 7-3.) Doing this for one or two rounds at the start of each workout helps ingrain the habit of maintaining proper foot placement, which in turn ensures that you remain balanced.

FIGURE 7-2: An agility ladder is a great tool for developing the proper footwork.

Courtesy of TITLE Boxing

Staying light as a dancer

The best boxers have always been able to glide effortlessly around the ring, although plodders such as Sonny Liston and George Foreman achieved great success because they were powerful punchers. But not too many of us can punch like Sonny or George, so the wiser option is to develop the ability to move lightly around the ring. This allows you to determine where the fight will be fought and forces your opponent to follow you.

FIGURE 7-3: A simple agility ladder drill to improve your footwork.

with permission of Anthony Policano

You use the natural spring in your legs to allow you to skip along the canvas until you get into a position to dig in and start punching. The way to do this is to balance mostly on the balls of your feet, knees slightly bent and legs loose. Rope skipping, which is covered in Chapter 6, will help you develop the spring in your step that you will need to do this effectively.

"Being ready to go anywhere, but not without a reason"

The preceding line is from the great boxing writer A.J. Liebling to describe the style of Archie Moore, a former light-heavyweight champion who posed a gallant challenge to Rocky Marciano's heavyweight title in 1955. Liebling was referring to Moore's economy of movement and awareness of where he was in the ring at all times. There's no point in moving just for the sake of movement. The idea is to keep the fight in areas where you're most effective. For example, Muhammad Ali was at his most effective when circling the perimeter of the ring and keeping his opponent in the center. Joe Frazier, on the other hand, preferred to pressure his opponents until they found themselves against the ropes, where he could do the most damage. Determining where you're most effective will come after a decent amount of sparring. The point is, once you've figured out where you want the fight to take place, stay disciplined with your movement in the ring to ensure it remains there.

The importance of staying grounded

Simply put, it's nearly impossible to deliver a truly hard punch with one or both of your feet off the floor. That's why, although it's important to remain light on your feet and ready to move when necessary, it's just as important to dig your feet into the canvas when throwing a punch, as shown in Figure 7-4. Since all punching power emanates from the legs and transmits to the fist through the rotation of the hips and torso, it stands to reason that the feet must be firmly anchored to the floor to execute this correctly. The correct way to do this is to be on the balls of your feet when moving but to dig in and push off on your heels when punching. Master this simple technique and you'll notice a huge difference in punching power.

FIGURE 7-4: Both feet need to be planted on the canvas to deliver a hard punch.

with permission of Anthony Policano

Discovering the Proper Way to Punch

Boxers have a unique way of punching unlike anything you see in the movies. This is not John Wayne-in-a-barroom-brawl, pulling his fist all the way back and clocking some poor victim who just stands there waiting to get clobbered. And it's not the type of punching you see in MMA matches, which is often delivered from the knees or with one or both feet off the ground. It is not a swing, a slap, or a flail. It is a piston-like movement that comes without warning and lands with a snapping thud.

A boxer's punch is short, concise, and, if delivered correctly, carries every ounce of the fighter's weight and transfers it to the fist. Believe it or not, this is not difficult to learn. With a little discipline and a lot of repetition, you too can learn to punch like a professional boxer. (See Figure 7-5.)

FIGURE 7-5: A diagram showing the proper technique for punching like a professional boxer.

A good way to understand the weight shift and the transfer of power is to think about how your car works. The wheels turn, providing motion, but they are not the source of the motion. The source of a car's power is its engine, and the means of transferring that power is its transmission. The wheels are just the last link in the chain.

Think of your fists as the equivalent of your car's wheels. Your engine is the weight of your body, and your transmission is what exercise physiologists call your *kinetic chain* — your legs, hips, core, shoulders, and arms — working together to transfer that weight to your fist, the last link in the body's kinetic chain. We must learn to coordinate that kinetic chain to produce short, concise, powerful punches.

Shooting straight from the shoulder

In boxing, the most effective punches are delivered straight from the shoulder. No looping, windmilling, or flailing. A snapshot taken at the end of a properly thrown punch should have you looking like a Greek statue, hip turned and arm fully extended at the same level of your shoulder on impact. (See Figure 7-6.)

FIGURE 7-6: Two views of how your body should look at the end of a well-delivered punch.

with permission of Anthony Policano

Now, let's go back to your high school physics class for a moment, shall we? Remember the lesson that said the shortest distance between two points is a straight line? That's the lesson that we as boxers must internalize and live by. Our punches, even our hooks, must land in a straight line from the middle of our bodies. The great former heavyweight champion Jack Dempsey called this the *power line* and he believed that punching along it was the secret to being a KO artist. He should know, having scored some of the most vicious KOs in boxing history.

The way to do this is by visualizing a vertical line bisecting your torso. Now project that line forward to your target, whether that's a heavy bag or an opponent. When you punch, you want your blows to land on or near that line. (See Figure 7-7.) And remember, the line moves with us, so if we maneuver to the left or right of our target, our punch will land in a different spot. This will become clear to you when dipping left or right to hit a specific spot on the bag or an opponent's body.

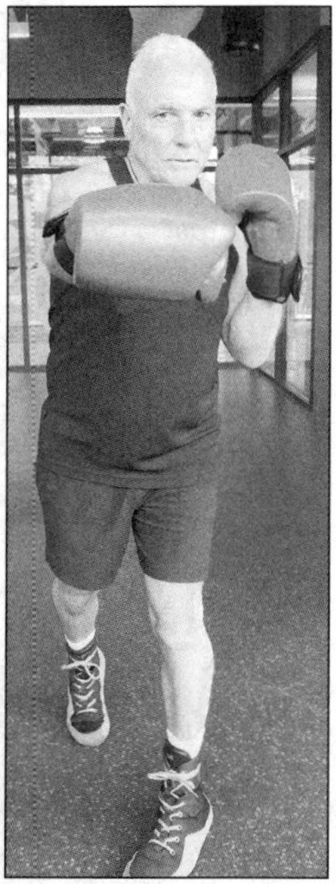

FIGURE 7-7: A right cross delivered along the power line.

with permission of Anthony Policano

The best way to keep your punches on the power line is to throw them straight from the shoulder, without looping. There is little power in a roundhouse punch because it strays from the power line. It is the coordinated movement of your kinetic chain that creates the power of the punch.

TIP

Aim to land your punches with the last two knuckles of your hand. If you hold your arm straight out, elbow locked, and visualize a line running from your shoulder to your fist, you will see that it runs right through the knuckle of your ring finger. This is the power line personified, and this is where your fist should impact its target.

For example, when throwing a jab (with your front hand), the kinetic chain begins with a half step forward with your front foot, which then causes a slight turn forward with your front hip and front shoulder, followed by a forward movement of your arm, and, finally, your fist. Try standing with your front hand forward in a boxing position — legs shoulder-width apart, knees slightly bent, hands up, palms facing one another with the dominant hand back, chin down, and body profiled to your opponent — and, without moving your arm, take a half step forward and rotate your front hip. You will see that your arm and hand automatically snap forward.

Now try it with your back, or power, hand (usually your dominant hand), only this time, instead of stepping forward with your back foot, violently rotate your back hip forward and pivot on the toes of your back foot as if you're crushing out a lit cigarette or grinding a bug into the carpet. (See Figure 7-8.) *Voilà!* Your back arm and fist will shoot forward as the last moving part in the kinetic chain.

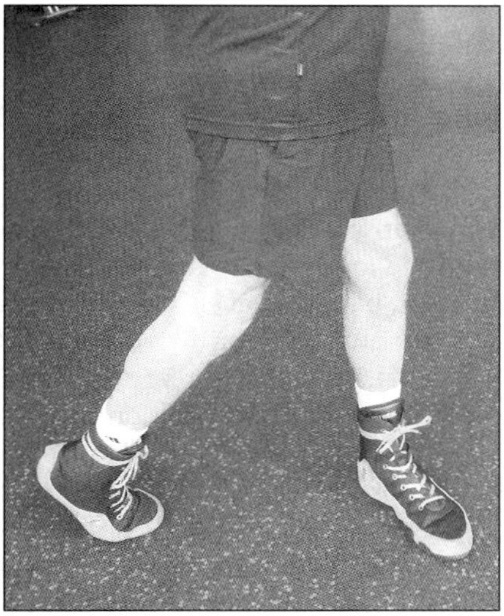

FIGURE 7-8: The hip turn and toe pivot when delivering a cross.

with permission of Anthony Policano

REMEMBER

Punching power often has little to do with muscularity. Some of the most formidable KO punchers in boxing — Thomas Hearns, Aaron Pryor, Alexis Arguello, Mark Breland — were not particularly muscular men. The average human arm weighs about 10 pounds and the average fist about 12 ounces. An arm punch carries little weight, no matter how muscular the arm. The true power of a punch comes from the transfer of body weight, and that comes with technique, not muscles.

Working on rotational punching and the weight shift

The technique described above is the basis of rotational punching, which results in the shifting of your body weight from your legs, through your hips and torso and into your fist. Hip rotation is the basis of generating power in many sports; most present-day Major League Baseball hitting coaches teach rotational hitting rather than the traditional stride toward the pitcher while swinging. Hip rotation has been found to generate more power and torque than simply stepping forward.

As described above, a good way to hone this movement is to assume your boxing stance and simply practice turning your hips without punching. As the movement becomes more comfortable you can let your arms go, loosely, with your hands open and without muscling up. You are aiming for fluidity of movement, not maximum effort. Once you achieve that, you'll find that power will follow. Proper punching is a matter of technique over strength.

Now, ball up those fists and practice the movement while adding torque to your punches. The way you do this is by beginning with your palms facing one another while in your starting position, and snapping them over so that your palms are facing the floor on impact. By "snapping" I mean rotating your fists violently in the air as the travel toward their target. This will add torque to the punch and you will hear and feel the effect when you strike a bag, a hand pad or an opponent. Start slowly at first, front hand followed by rear hand. As the movement becomes more natural, increase the speed, but remember to reset yourself into your starting position after each set of two punches. For instance, if you're a right-handed boxer with your right (dominant) hand to the rear, you would throw your left, your right, and then return to your starting position of hands up, chin down, knees slightly bent, and feet shoulder-width apart. Rinse and repeat as many times as necessary for the movement to feel fluid and natural to you.

You will use a similar movement when throwing your hook. In boxing, the hook is generally thrown only with the front hand. The proper way to do it is to pivot on the ball of your front foot and twist your torso to the right while keeping your front arm in an L-shape. (See Figure 7-9.) It's not a swing or a roundhouse, but a power punch that is delivered close to your body when fighting inside. It's a very similar motion to slamming a door in anger.

There are two ways you can throw your hook: with your fist in the same position as if holding a coffee cup, or with your palm down facing the floor. (See Figure 7-10.)

FIGURE 7-9: The proper form for throwing your hook. Your arm is in an L-shape.

with permission of Anthony Policano

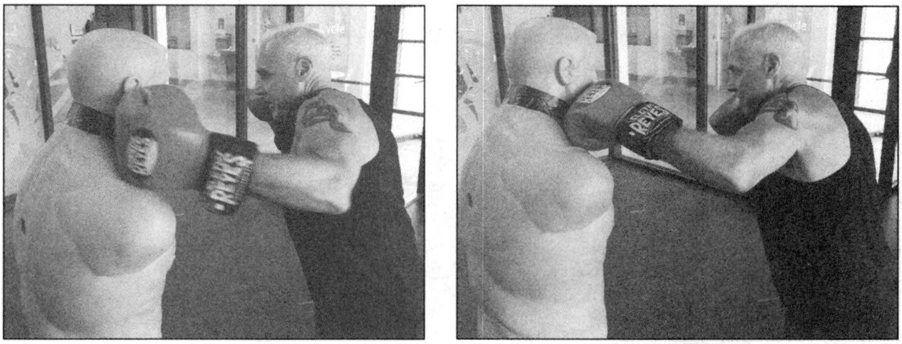

FIGURE 7-10: The hook delivered with the palm perpendicular to the floor (left) and the palm down (right).

with permission of Anthony Policano

I prefer the palm-down method because I think it adds a little more snap to the punch, but you should use the method that feels more comfortable to you. Whichever method you prefer, your fist should impact its target straight on within the power line. This technique is described in greater detail in Chapter 9.

The importance of gauging your distance

Now that you've begun to master how to throw a punch, the next thing to learn is how to land a punch without getting hit by your opponent. The first step in that process is to understand how far away you must be from your target to land with optimal impact. The correct distance for a boxer will vary depending upon their body type, arm length, and fighting style. For instance, a long-armed boxer such as Muhammad Ali, Larry Holmes, or Thomas Hearns — each of whom was reliant on a jab to set up their other punches — needs to be a little further away from an opponent to get full extension on their punches. Shorter-armed fighters such as Joe Frazier and Mike Tyson need to be closer because they rely upon hooks and body shots to do most of their damage.

A fighter such as Ali would find his punches *smothered*, that is, lacking power and snap, if he was too close to his opponent. Likewise, Frazier or Tyson would find their punches falling short, leaving them open for counterpunches, if they were too far away.

A good way to judge the proper distance for you is on the heavy bag. If you are the long-armed jabbing type, you should fully extend your jabbing arm so that your fist just touches the surface of the bag. (See Figure 7-11.) When you take your step with the jab, you'll find that the punch will land with the proper amount of snap and power. That's about where you want to be in relation to your chosen target, be it bag or boxer. Then immediately return to your starting position with your hands up and your chin down. The mechanics of delivering a sharp, snappy jab are covered in greater detail in Chapter 8.

FIGURE 7-11: Start gauging your distance by extending your jabbing arm until it just touches your target.

with permission of Anthony Policano

If you're a shorter-armed hooking type of fighter, you should position yourself close enough to land those hooks with full power, but not so close that the fist impacts the bag with more of a pushing motion than a snap. You will know from the way the punch feels and the way it sounds if you are at the right distance. Also, if your punch lands correctly, the bag will not move very much. If it does, your hook was more of a push than a punch.

Once you've established the proper distance for your punches, you must remember that you've also got to be far enough away not to get hit back. For the long-armed boxer, that means taking a half step back while keeping your hands up and moving your head from side to side. For the short-armed boxer, it means getting low and rolling your upper body from side to side without giving ground, while keeping your hands up.

REMEMBER

It's dangerous for a long-armed boxer to be too close to their opponent. Conversely, it's dangerous for a short-armed boxer to be too far away from their opponent. Both mistakes put the boxer right into their opponent's punching range.

Always return to square one

It's imperative for all boxers, regardless of the style they choose to box with, to reset their position repeatedly throughout a fight or a workout. The reset is when the boxer adjusts the position of their feet, brings the fists back up into guarding position, and takes a deep breath or two before launching another attack. (See Figure 7-12.)

I'm sure I sound like a broken record in my classes because I am constantly reminding my clients to reset themselves after each combination. In a boxing match, professional boxers are not constantly punching; they are assessing the situation in front of them, jockeying for position, trying to find the right angles from which to punch, concentrating on defense, and, most importantly, breathing in between exchanges.

TIP

Since breathing comes naturally to all of us it may seem elementary to say this, but the proper way to breathe is in through the nose and out through the mouth, and in any strenuous endeavor, to exhale on exertion. For instance, when bench pressing, you inhale when the barbell is on the way down and exhale forcefully when pushing it up. In boxing, it means inhaling through your nose when not punching and exhaling hard through the mouth with each punch. That's why you often hear grunting sounds when boxers deliver a blow.

with permission of Anthony Policano

FIGURE 7-12: Remember to always return to your starting position — hands up, chin down — after delivering a punch or combination.

IN THIS CHAPTER

» Establishing your jab

» Snapping your way to victory

» Setting up your power shots

» Power punching with your cross

Chapter 8

Learning the Ol' One-Two

The combination of jab and cross — known colloquially as "the ol' one-two" — is the most elemental of punch combinations, as basic to boxing as the fastball and curve are to baseball. But while it sounds like a simple skill to master, learning to throw it correctly takes practice and attention to detail. If you are new to boxing training, this is where it all begins. And like any other discipline, before you get into anything truly complex, you've got to learn your ABCs. The jab and cross are boxing's A and B.

Respecting the Power of the Jab

Jack Dempsey, the former heavyweight champion of the Roaring '20s, had little use for the jab.

He considered the punch "futile" and ineffective as used by the fighters of the '40s and '50s. "They tap, they slap, they flick, they paw, they paint. Most of them couldn't knock your hat off with their left jabs," Dempsey wrote in his book *Championship Fighting: Explosive Punching and Aggressive Defense*, published in 1950.

Dempsey preferred to refer to his version of the punch as a "left jolt," thrown with full body weight behind it and intended not to set up a knockout punch, but to *be* a knockout punch.

Far be it from me to argue with the Manassa Mauler, one of the most powerful and ferocious heavyweight champions in boxing history and the first true superstar professional athlete, but on this point, I must take issue. Unless you can punch like Dempsey — or Joe Frazier or Mike Tyson, two other heavyweights with similar disdain for the punch — the jab should be an essential part of your toolbox.

Whether you use a conventional (right-handed) stance or fight southpaw, the jab might be the most important punch in your arsenal. It is similar to a baseball pitcher's fastball in that it sets up everything else that you throw. And like the fastball in a pitcher's repertoire, the jab is number one, the party of the first part in "the ol' one-two."

REMEMBER

Once you establish your jab, it becomes easier to land your power shots. A jab can be used to keep your opponent at bay, gauge your distance, buy time if you're tiring, and create openings for your power punches, most notably your cross. I tell my clients to think of their jab as knocking on the door — "Anybody home? Anybody home?" — and when the door opens, to crash through it with a hard, straight cross. Other analogies I have used in teaching the jab are "sending the dogs out to see what they bring back" and doing exploratory surgery. All mean basically the same thing: The jab is a probing punch, not a KO blow; it is designed to clear the way for bigger things to come. With apologies to Jack Dempsey, of course.

Imagining a brick at the end of a two-by-four

Just because the jab is basically a setup punch doesn't mean it can't have some sting behind it. The jab of former heavyweight champion Larry Holmes was said to be more powerful than many boxers' crosses, and you need only look at the damage done to Joe Frazier in his classic trilogy with Muhammad Ali to know that there was something behind Ali's jabs as well. I tell my students to visualize their jab as a brick attached to the end of a two-by-four, the image of a good, stiff punch that carries a bit of a wallop.

TIP

The trick to an effective jab is to make sure you are transferring weight behind your jab by pushing off the ball of your back foot and taking a half-step forward with your front foot while snapping your fist forward with authority. Don't jab with an open hand or a loose wrist, and don't backhand it. Keep your fist closed tightly and send it out straight from the shoulder, with no telegraphing, pullback, or really any clue at all that the jab is coming. And make sure your jabbing hand and front foot move together; otherwise, you'll throw yourself off-balance and be open for a counter shot.

Dancing the step-and-jab two-step

The jab is always thrown with the front hand, meaning if you are a right-handed boxer, you will stand with your left foot forward and jab with your left hand. If you are a left-handed boxer, you will do the reverse.

To throw the jab properly, begin in your basic fighting stance with your hands up — front hand slightly lower than your eyes, back hand up around your ear — and your palms facing inward. (See Figure 8-1.) As you deliver the punch, you should twist your fist, fast and hard, so that on impact your palm is facing downward. This twist puts added torque on your jab, which increases its snap. The correct way to jab includes a half-step forward with your front foot, with your fist just a few inches beyond that foot on impact. The foot and fist should move simultaneously. (See Figure 8-2.)

FIGURE 8-1: The fist and foot move together when jabbing.

with permission of Anthony Policano

FIGURE 8-2: How you should look at the end of your jab: fist palm down and arm at full extension.

with permission of Anthony Policano

REMEMBER

If you don't take that step, you are likely to throw yourself off-balance and leave yourself vulnerable to a counter.

And after you have thrown the jab, be sure to step back into your regular starting stance and pull your jabbing hand straight back into a guarding position. Don't let it drop around your waist or, again, you run the risk of getting tagged with a counterpunch. At the same time, be conscious of the position of your back hand; it should remain up alongside your head at about the level of your ear.

TIP

I tell my students to imagine they are holding a cellphone with one hand while jabbing with the other. That seems to be an image everyone can conjure up these days. The best way to master this is to practice your jab in front of a mirror, both facing forward and watching yourself from the side. It will be easy to see whether you are fully extending your arm, whether your foot and fist are moving together, and, most importantly, whether you are dropping either of your hands.

Working on your snap, crackle, pop

I keep using the word "snap" for a reason. The only truly effective punches in boxing are "snapped," not pushed. That means not only minimizing the time between the beginning of the punch and its impact, but also minimizing the time between its impact and its return to the guarding position. This is best illustrated by jabbing at the heavy bag. If the bag swings on impact, you are pushing it. If it stays virtually stationary and you hear a sharp crack, you are snapping it.

REMEMBER

As in all boxing techniques, perfecting your jab will take practice, practice, and more practice. In this game, repetition makes perfect. And remember — twist your fist so that your palm faces downward on impact. That will impart the snap you're looking for.

Using your jab to set up your power shots

The most important function of a good jab is to create openings for your power shots to both the head and the body — namely your crosses (right hand if you're a right-handed boxer, left if you're a lefty) and your hooks (like the jab, thrown with the front hand) to both the head and body. The one-two may be the oldest combination in boxing, but it remains one of the most effective. It is generally thrown after a couple of setup jabs; when the opening is there, the jab and cross are delivered virtually simultaneously, with the jab momentarily blinding your opponent and the cross administering the coup de grâce.

TIP

An example of a perfect one-two resulting in a knockout was thrown by Thomas Hearns in a 1986 fight against James Shuler — a fight that lasted less than a minute. Study that one if you want to know how it should be done. (The video is readily available on the Internet; you might try `www.youtube.com/watch?v=p8rLHcnNEC4`.)

FIGHTING WORDS

Larry Holmes, possessor of possibly the best jab in heavyweight boxing history, described the effect of his one-two thusly: "First I get 'em drunk [with the jab] and then I mug 'em [with the right cross]."

The jab is also effective in setting up the hook, either to the head or to the body. "Hooking off the jab" is an advanced technique but one well worth mastering. It involves delivering a snappy jab and then, without pause, following with a hook thrown with the same hand. This combination will take a lot of practice because it requires a hard turn of the upper body and a short, tight hook; otherwise, you will telegraph the second punch and likely get hit by a countering cross. The jab can also set up a hook to the body. The way to do it is to jab to the head and then dip your body slightly to your jabbing side while violently rotating your hips. The result will be a powerful hook to the midsection. We will get into the mechanics of properly delivering a hook both to the head and to the body in Chapter 9.

TIP

Once again, Thomas Hearns was a master at both these techniques. You can learn much by studying his fights, even the few he lost.

Don't faint — *feint!*

In addition to being the art of self-defense and the art of self-control, boxing is also the art of deception: *Look at this hand while I hit you with that hand.* The great former light-heavyweight champion Jose Torres used to say that to be a great boxer, one must be a great liar. They must lie to their opponents about not being tired, or hurt, or scared, or discouraged. And they must lie about what they plan to do in the course of the fight. In a lot of ways, a fight is a misdirection play, and there are a lot of tactics you can use to try to deceive your opponent into doing what you want them to do.

One of the most effective tactics you can use to set up your jab is the feint, which is nothing more than a fake punch designed to draw your opponent into committing themselves and thereby leaving an opening for a counter. The simplest way to feint is to fake your jab — start it but don't let it go — which often causes your opponent either to flinch or to move toward you, either of which will give you an opening to land a punch.

You can also feint by slightly dropping your front shoulder — a tactic Buster Douglas used effectively in his shocking 1990 upset over Mike Tyson — to draw reaction; by faking a punch to the midsection and then rapidly bringing your fist up to your opponent's head; or even by simply moving your eyes to one part of your opponent's anatomy while hitting them in another.

Pro tip: Practice your feints against the heavy bag before trying them in the ring against a real opponent.

Crossing Over with the Cross: Developing Your Money Punch

Having an effective jab — or "an educated left," as the old-timers would say — is extremely important, but it's little more than an annoyance to your opponent if there's nothing coming behind it. A jab without a follow-up power shot is basically all windup and no pitch, so to speak. That's where your cross comes in. Learning how to throw it correctly is essential to a boxer. *Imagine a bowling ball at the end of an I-beam.*

The cross is the party of the second part in the ol' one-two. It is thrown with your rear hand, off your back foot, with a full rotation of your rear hip and a pivot on your back foot, similar to the way you would move when swinging a baseball bat or a tennis racket or a golf club.

To throw the cross correctly, sit back on your rear foot slightly so most of your weight is on that leg. This is the loading phase. (See Figure 8-3.)

Then comes the pivot. I used to describe that pivot to my clients as akin to grinding out a cigarette butt under your foot but since (thankfully) fewer people smoke nowadays, I prefer to describe it as crushing a bug on your kitchen floor.

This hip turn and toe pivot transfers all your body weight to your fist, through the power line of your torso. And, like the jab, your fist should be twisted in the air so that it lands with your palm facing downward to increase the snap in the punch. (See Figures 8-4, 8-5, and 8-6.)

FIGURE 8-3: The position of your body just before unloading your cross.

with permission of Anthony Policano

REMEMBER

If you do all this correctly — and it will take some practice — the cross will be a power punch in your arsenal, a bowling ball at the end of a steel beam. Take a look at Rocky Marciano's one-punch KO of Jersey Joe Walcott to win the heavyweight title in 1951 and you'll understand what I mean. (Again, that knockout punch is easy to find on the Internet; try `www.youtube.com/watch?v=npz7kFB4Vo4`.)

FIGURE 8-4: The hip turn is essential for transferring your body weight when throwing your cross.

with permission of Anthony Policano

FIGURE 8-5: Punch right through the bag with your follow-through.

with permission of Anthony Policano

FIGURE 8-6: The cross at full extension.

with permission of Anthony Policano

Learn to throw it correctly

The cross is generally thrown with one's dominant hand, meaning if you're right-handed and fighting out of a traditional left leg forward stance, you'll throw it with your right hand, and if you're fighting southpaw (right leg forward), you'll throw it with your left.

REMEMBER

Obviously, there are exceptions to every rule; two of the greatest fighters in history, Joe Frazier and Oscar de la Hoya, were left-handed but fought out of right-handed stances, and both Marvelous Marvin Hagler and Terence (Bud) Crawford seemed equally comfortable in either stance.

The cross should be thrown straight as an arrow, from the shoulder, starting with the fist held up in guarding position. (Remember to hold that rear hand up as if you were talking on your cellphone while boxing!) Do not loop the punch or swing it overhand like a baseball pitcher; both moves will rob the punch of some (if not all) of its power and leave you open to a counterpunch.

TIP

Visualize your crossing arm and fist as a piston, shooting straight out and returning straight back to its original position. (See Figure 8-7.) Or, if you prefer, like the spring-loaded plunger on a pinball machine, which shoots out and comes right back to where it started. That way you do not compromise your defense, because your rear hand is largely responsible for picking off or parrying your opponent's jab.

The cross is generally delivered to the head of your opponent, but it can also be effective to the body — and especially to the solar plexus, if you duck down while delivering it. (See Figure 8-7.) Another effective use of the cross is to double it, ducking down to hit the body and immediately straightening up to drive it to the head. But wherever you throw it, your cross needs to be delivered powerfully and with snap. This is your money punch.

FIGURE 8-7: Delivering a hard right cross to the solar plexus.

with permission of Anthony Policano

Leading with your right (or left, if you're a southpaw)

You can also throw your cross as a lead punch, meaning you will not set it up first with your jab. Muhammad Ali made great use of his lead right against Joe Frazier in their second and third fights and in his incredible knockout of George Foreman, considered unbeatable at the time, in the fight known as the Rumble in the Jungle. The lead cross can be a dangerous punch, however, because it exposes you to a possible counter. That is why it needs to be thrown sparingly, with great snap. It can also be effectively camouflaged by feinting first with your jabbing hand. Sometimes that millisecond of delay can cause your opponent to freeze, creating an opening for a lead with your crossing hand.

TIP

Like the jab, the cross is best developed on the heavy bag, either behind your jab (there's that ol' one-two again) or as a lead punch. In throwing the one-two, the jab and cross should land virtually simultaneously, with the jab creating the opening and the cross plowing through. When throwing the lead cross, again, speed and snap are essential, as is quickly pulling that hand back into guarding position. In either case, you must practice and perfect the hip turn and foot pivot to ensure the maximum power in the punch.

Countering with the Counterpunch: Make 'Em Miss, Make 'Em Pay

Your cross can also be a highly effective counterpunch, especially against an opponent's jab. The way to do it is to slip the incoming jab over your front shoulder by dipping your body to the right. That will position you safely out of the way of your opponent's cross. You then snap your crossing hand to your opponent's (presumably) unprotected jaw. (See Figure 8-8.) I delve into the specifics of slipping punches in the chapter on defense, but understand that slipping a punch is simply moving your head from side to side, allowing the punch to sail harmlessly past its target. This takes a lot of practice and concentration in sparring or a fight, because it requires you to watch your opponent closely to correctly time the jab. But you can work on this on the heavy bag or the double-end bag, by first jabbing at it, and then dipping away from the imaginary punch (toward the side of your crossing hand) before delivering your own cross. Do this repeatedly on both bags before trying it against an opponent!

REMEMBER

When you slip a punch, you needn't make it miss by very much. A quarter-inch will do. Don't make your sideways movement too exaggerated or you will move out of position to throw an effective counter.

There is another way to use your cross as a counterpunch, and that is by catching your opponent's jabbing hand with your open glove and then responding with a cross over it. This, too, is an advanced move that can only really be perfected in the ring against an opponent, or with a coach during a mitt work session. This is covered in more detail in Chapter 10.

FIGURE 8-8: A counter right cross can be delivered after slipping a jab over your right shoulder.

with permission of Anthony Policano

IN THIS CHAPTER

» Punching with power

» Learning the hook

» Mastering the uppercut

Chapter 9

The Wrecking Crew: Hooks, Uppercuts, and Body Shots

Mastering the jab and cross is an essential skill for any boxer, but to be truly effective in the ring, you've got to be able to get your opponent's attention. That means punching with power. (Of course, the cross, as documented in Chapter 8, is a power punch as well.) The plain truth is, if you can't get your opponent's respect for your punching power, there's little you can do to hold them off, besides run. And the boxing ring is a small area. You'll find that you run out of room in a hurry. As the great heavyweight champion Joe Louis observed before his fight with the speedy Billy Conn, "He can run, but he can't hide." Louis was right, of course; Conn, who was winning the fight largely through his foot speed, ran out of running room in the 13th round of their first bout and was knocked out. He simply didn't have enough punching power to hold the relentless Louis off for the entire fight.

That's why it's important to be more than just a Fancy Dan in the ring. You have to give your opponent a reason *not* to rush into your punches, or walk through them. You want the other person in that ring to realize that discretion is the better part of valor when fighting you, and that any action they take will be met with an equal or greater reaction from you.

And even if your plans do not include actually stepping into the ring to fight someone, you will find it immensely satisfying to be able to hit the bags or the hand pads with real power during your workouts. There is a rewarding *crack!* that comes with a solid impact, and you'll find that hard punching, especially against a heavy bag, is a wonderful shoulder developer.

So let's get punching.

TIP

Before we start power punching, please note that all punches should land on the last three knuckles of your fist: the middle, ring, and little fingers. That area of your fist is the final link in the power line of your body, which begins in your legs and runs through your hips, shoulders, and arms. Get into the habit of landing your punches on that part of your fist, not on the pinky or index finger.

The Hook: Boxing's Most Devastating Weapon

Great boxers from Jack Dempsey to Smokin' Joe Frazier to Sugar Ray Leonard and countless others have relied on the hook to subdue and often stop their opponents. Some examples of great hooks include the one Dempsey floored Jess Willard with in the first round of their 1919 heavyweight title bout, the hook Frazier dropped Muhammad Ali with in the 15th round of their transcendent 1971 fight, and the hook Leonard employed to ferocious effect against the much bigger Donny Lalonde in their 1988 super-middleweight title bout. Even Ali, renowned more as an incredibly fast and flashy boxer than a puncher, used a series of powerful hooks to knock out Oscar Bonavena, a tough heavyweight contender, in their 1970 non-title bout.

The hook is also probably the punch most often thrown incorrectly. Figures 9-1 and 9-2 illustrate the proper form for throwing an effective hook.

REMEMBER

In boxing, the hook is *always* thrown with the front (jabbing) hand. Other disciplines, and many boxing exercise classes, teach hooking with both hands but I do not teach my clients to throw a hook with their rear hand. In a match against a skilled boxer, a hook thrown from that position would be seen a mile away and easily countered. I consider it an amateurish punch that offends my sense of correct boxing form. So we don't do it.

FIGURE 9-1: The starting position for delivering a proper hook. The weight is on your front foot and your body is leaning slightly toward your hooking hand.

with permission of Anthony Policano

FIGURE 9-2: The mid-point of a well-delivered hook, and then bingo! The hook finds its target.

with permission of Anthony Policano

Thrown correctly, the hook is a short punch delivered while close to your opponent. It's not a swing; your hooking arm should not venture wide of your body. Not only will this rob the punch of much of its force as it strays from your body's power line, but it will leave you wide open for a straight counterpunch. Remember your high school geometry: The shortest distance between two points is a straight line. If you swing your hook, you will surely get beaten to the punch by a straight shot.

REMEMBER

Since most boxers, and people, are right-handed, you are probably more familiar with the term "left hook." But the same principles that apply to the hook for a right-handed boxer also work for the southpaw, who jabs with the right hand, and thus hooks with it as well.

The hook: Throwing it Jack Dempsey style

Dempsey, the heavyweight champion of the world from 1919 to 1926, was a devastating left hooker who delivered the punch in a unique way, so that his fist contacted the target straight on rather than from the side. Dempsey touted a concept he called the "power line," an imaginary line that bisected the body vertically and from where he believed all punching power flowed. Consequently, he kept his punches close to his body, believing, rightly, that "swinging" negated the weight transfer and reduced the power to an arm punch.

To throw the Dempsey hook, take a short step to your right while keeping your hooking arm in an L-shape. Turn your fist and elbow over sharply as you deliver the blow so that your palm is parallel to the floor. Aim for the center of your target, be it a heavy bag, a torso bag, or your opponent's face. (See Figure 9-3.) Follow through as if you're trying to hit your target with your elbow. But don't actually do it: Elbowing is a foul.

The hook: Throwing it Joe Frazier style

Frazier, who held the heavyweight title from 1970 to 1973, cemented his greatest victory with the left hook that floored Muhammad Ali in the 15th round of their first meeting in 1971. That punch was an unorthodox variety of hook — the 5-11 Frazier literally left his feet to connect with the 6-3 Ali — and it impacted the side of Ali's jaw. To the untrained eye, it looks like a swing more than a punch, and the antithesis of the Dempsey hook.

This version of the hook is not for everyone. Frazier came by it naturally since he was left-handed but fought in a right-handed stance. And a boyhood accident had left him unable to fully straighten his left arm, leaving it in a permanent L-shape, the optimal position for a hook. His motion was loose but violent; he whipped his hook around with blinding speed, generating a lot of power to both the head and body. If you watch a video of his fight with George Foreman, in which he lost his title on a KO, you'll see that with his back to the ropes, Frazier hooks so violently that he hits the rope behind him with his fist.

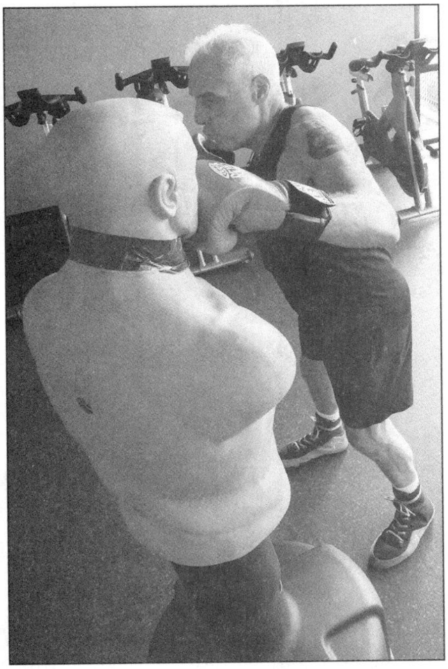

FIGURE 9-3: The Dempsey hook hits its target straight on.

with permission of Anthony Policano

Certainly, Frazier's hook worked for him and there are times when you will want to aim your hook at the side of a bag or an opponent's head or body. (See Figure 9-4.) But be aware that it's also a risky punch, because it's longer than the Dempsey hook and leaves the hooker vulnerable to a straight counterblow. Not many fighters were fast or brave enough to stand in and counter Frazier's hook, but Ali, with his lightning-fast reflexes, was able to score repeatedly with his right hand as Frazier wound up his hook. So use it with discretion.

Whichever way you choose to throw it, the most efficient way to deliver a hook is by violently twisting your upper body while keeping your hooking arm in that L-shaped configuration, elbow up and palm down. This takes some practice. Most beginners find it awkward and tend to swing the punch in the fashion of a slap. You must keep your elbow tight to your body when throwing the hook. And depending upon your foot placement, the punch may land either to the side of your opponent's head, or straight on to the face. Either way, if you execute the rotational weight shift correctly, it will be a powerful punch.

FIGURE 9-4: The Frazier hook homes in from the side.

with permission of Anthony Policano

To practice the proper form, take your stance relatively close to the heavy bag or torso bag and repeatedly drive your fist into it, being careful to turn your body hard, snap your elbow up, and turn your palm over on impact. Practice hitting the bag or torso in both spots: the side of the head and straight on into the face. When you've mastered that, you can then move on to the double-end or cobra bag and practice hitting them with multiple hooks. This takes a lot of repetition, but when you can do that consistently, you'll have added a very important weapon to your arsenal.

The hook to the body is another vital skill to master. I cover it in detail in the section on body punching.

TIP

When throwing a hook, repeat this mantra to yourself: *More body, less arm.* Translated, it means don't swing your arm when hooking. Rotate your upper body to effectively transfer your weight to your fist — it's a short, less pronounced rotation than when throwing a cross, for instance — and deliver the punch with a motion similar to slamming a door in anger. (See Figure 9-5.)

FIGURE 9-5: Don't swing your hook! This is sure to get you countered. Keep it short and tight.

with permission of Anthony Policano

The Uppercut: Sneaky and Deadly

The uppercut is the wrecking ball of punches. It's unlike any of the other punches we've learned so far, because unlike the jab, cross, and hook, it's not delivered straight from the shoulder, but up from the floor. Besides the fact that it, too, carries the full weight of the body if thrown correctly, the uppercut is especially effective because it's difficult, if not impossible, to see it coming.

Some of boxing's most devastating KOs have been the result of perfectly thrown uppercuts. And at least one of boxing's most shocking losses was the result of a poorly thrown uppercut. To see examples of the former, check out the uppercut George Foreman drops Joe Frazier with in their 1973 title bout (at 18 seconds left in the first round; `https://www.youtube.com/watch?v=QjOxjPE_14g`), or the casual, walking uppercut with which Foreman knocked out Gerry Cooney in 1990 (`https://www.youtube.com/shorts/laK8lEnvBts`). Larry Holmes also used an uppercut to save his title from a stiff challenge from Mike (Hercules) Weaver in 1979 (`https://www.youtube.com/shorts/4S43uI4uzdk`).

REMEMBER

On the flip side, Buster Douglas, in his first title defense after his shocking 1990 upset over Mike Tyson, lost his title when he badly missed a wild right uppercut and was promptly KO'd by Evander Holyfield's perfectly timed counter right (`https://www.youtube.com/shorts/K98a9TT1ozk`). Clearly, the uppercut can be a double-edged sword, dangerous to both the fighter catching it, and the one throwing it. So take care when throwing it and use it sparingly.

The uppercut is generally thrown with the rear hand, although it can also be thrown with the front hand, usually to the body. Throwing it with the rear hand involves dipping the body toward the side of the rear hand, to the right for right-handed boxers and to the left for southpaws, bending your knees slightly (the "load") and then snapping your body and fist upward, as in Figure 9-6. Usually, an uppercut thrown this way is intended to hit the point of the chin, although it can also be aimed at the solar plexus. It is imperative to keep your chin down and your front hand up in guarding position when throwing the uppercut or you run the risk of ending up like Douglas against Holyfield. The uppercut is a difficult punch to practice on the heavy bag, because your fist will almost invariably slide off the surface of the bag. It is best practiced either on a torso bag (see Figure 9-6) or a specially made uppercut bag, which is cylindrical like the heavy bag but hangs horizontally rather than vertically. You can also practice uppercuts on a double-end or cobra bag but you will find this an advanced technique that requires you to perfect the punch on the other bags first.

Throwing an uppercut with the front hand is slightly different. Here, too, you must dip your body and bend your knees to load the punch, but rather than

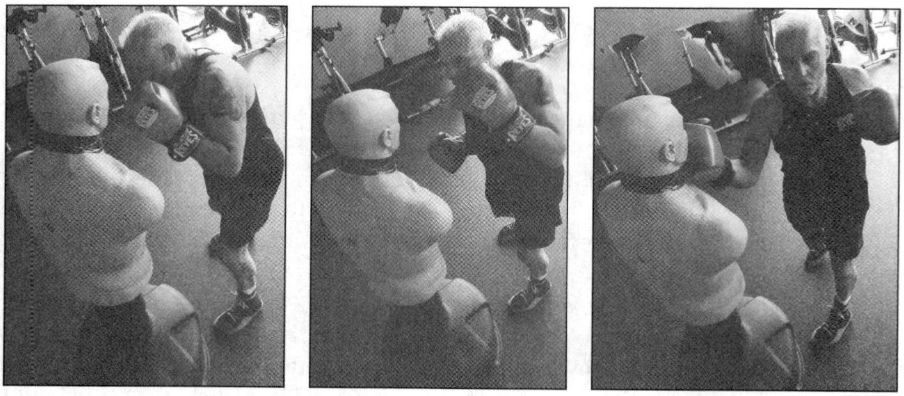

FIGURE 9-6: The mechanics of delivering the uppercut. Remember to keep your front hand up for protection!

with permission of Anthony Policano

coming straight up with your fist, I teach my clients to deliver the punch at close to a 45-degree angle, sort of a half-uppercut, half-hook. This punch, sometimes referred to as a "shovel hook," is more effective to the body than to the head.

Like the hook, you must be close to your opponent to throw the uppercut safely. Too far outside and you will likely miss the punch and leave yourself wide open. The uppercut is best delivered while infighting and as I mentioned earlier, used sparingly when the opportunity presents itself. If you're fighting an opponent who tends to duck punches, the uppercut can be an excellent weapon. Conversely, it's not easy to safely and effectively throw an uppercut against a taller fighter or a stand-up boxer who rarely fights from a crouch. These are the kinds of observations and judgments a fighter must make during the course of a fight, another reason why it's essential to remain calm and unemotional in the ring.

Gut Punching: Hitting 'Em Where They Live

The great heavyweight champion Joe Louis was once advised to attack an upcoming opponent in the body. "He doesn't like it there," the person advising Louis observed.

Louis's retort was as short and sweet as one of his trademark combinations: "Who do?"

The answer is nobody. Body punches sap an opponent's strength, take away their wind, and in at least one famous instance, caused the heavyweight title to suddenly change hands. That occurred on March 17, 1897, in Carson City, Nevada, when James J. (Gentleman Jim) Corbett, by all accounts winning a fight handily over Bob Fitzsimmons, suddenly went down and, although fully conscious, could not get up after taking a left hook to the body in the 14th round.

The shot became famous as "The Solar Plexus Punch," and for years I wondered how a fighter could lose his title over so innocuous-looking a blow. That is, until I got hit in the same spot by a mediocre-punching sparring partner as a 19-year-old Golden Glover. The punch didn't just hurt; it paralyzed me. Like Corbett, I too was fully conscious. And also — probably like Corbett — I honestly felt as if I were about to die. Down on all fours, I could not get my lungs or my legs to work. I couldn't rise and I couldn't breathe. Forget about beating a 10-count. I would not have beaten a 30-count.

That was when I fully realized the value of a strong, pinpointed body attack, as well as a concentrated exercise regime to tighten up my midsection. In truth, however, nothing can tighten up the solar plexus, the small triangle just beneath the breastbone where it meets the diaphragm. (See Figure 9-7.) If you doubt me, just jab two fingers into that area right now. I'll wait.

The solar plexus is just one of several vulnerable areas in the torso that can be effectively attacked by body shots. The short ribs on either side of the ribcage are a prime target (see Figure 9-8), as is the area of the sternum about midway up the chest. Sparring with a professional heavyweight with a losing record, I once got hit there so hard that I swear my heart and lungs vibrated. I would take 10 shots to the head over another one of those any day.

Sadly, body punching has become something of a lost art among today's boxers. Why? Several reasons.

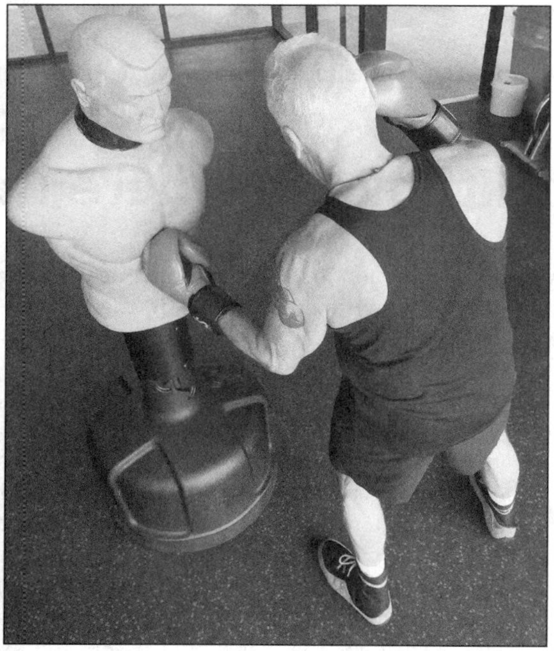

FIGURE 9-7: Practice hitting the solar plexus area of a torso bag. It's a fight-ender.

with permission of Anthony Policano

FIGURE 9-8: Aim for the floating ribs on a torso bag with your hook to the body.

with permission of Anthony Policano

For one thing, their effect is not always immediate and, the Corbett-Fitzsimmons example aside, they rarely produce knockouts or even knockdowns. It takes time and effort to wear down a well-trained opponent with a body attack. It's similar to putting a portion of your paycheck into a retirement account. It will eventually pay dividends, but you need to have patience.

For another, boxing judges have historically given less weight to body punches than to head shots. In fairness, they're more difficult to see clearly, especially if the judge is positioned behind the fighter being hit by them. And in all honesty, a lot of judges don't really know what they're watching or what's really happening in a fight.

Third, throwing body punches can be risky if not done correctly. A poorly thrown body punch, with the head up or without dipping the body first, can leave a boxer wide open to a counterpunch. A lot of fighters would rather not take the chance. And that's a shame, because especially in a long fight, a concentrated body attack can pay huge dividends in the later rounds. Ask Muhammad Ali, who urinated blood and whose hips were sore and swollen for days after taking 15 rounds of body shots from Joe Frazier in their first fight. Better yet, seek out the video and watch it for yourself.

Most body shots are short hooks, thrown with either hand and with a slight upward motion, your palm turned at about a 45-degree angle as the fist lands. (See Figure 9-9.) Jack Dempsey called these "shovel hooks" because of the upward angle of the punch.

You can also deliver straight punches to the body, generally with your rear hand and usually after having ducked or slipped under your opponent's jab, as shown in Figure 9-10.

While it may seem elementary to mention, when throwing body punches, it's essential to be close to your opponent. You cannot launch a shot to your opponent's midsection from the same position you would deliver a jab, for instance. That's just begging to be hit with a counterpunch. And you must also bend from the waist, keep your chin tucked in, and deliver your punches with the palm of your fist up, or at a 45-degree angle to the ground. It's generally best to begin a body attack with your lead hand, and not advised to throw more than four body punches at a time — preferably two and get out, or two to the body followed by a hook to the head. And after delivering the blows, you must back out while moving your head in a side-to-side motion. Pull straight back and you are presenting a very inviting target to your opponent.

FIGHTING WORDS

Fighters often refer to a flurry to the body as "shoeshining," because when delivered correctly, the movement of the fists resembles to action of buffing a pair of shoes with a cloth.

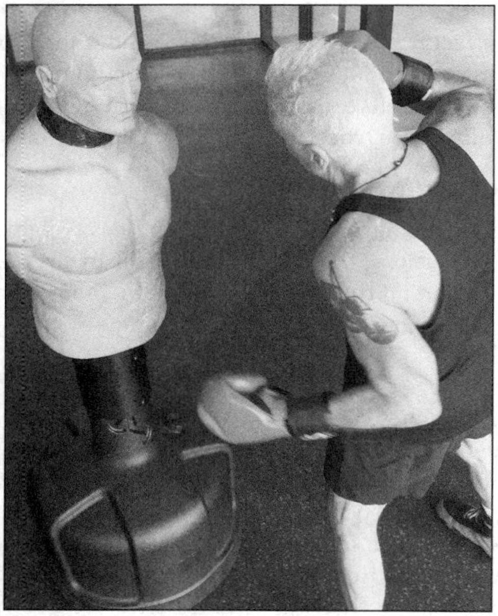

FIGURE 9-9: A so-called "shovel hook" delivered to the body with the front hand.

with permission of Anthony Policano

FIGURE 9-10: A straight punch delivered to the body with the rear hand.

with permission of Anthony Policano

4 Master Class

IN THIS PART . . .

Use footwork to avoid your opponent's punches and land your own.

Go forward, backward, and side to side to create punching angles.

Use your gloves to block your opponent's punches and set up counterpunches.

Defend yourself while leaving your hands free to punch.

IN THIS CHAPTER

» Learning to float like a butterfly

» Gauging (and keeping) your distance

» Advancing on the enemy

» Fighting in retreat

» Cutting off the ring

» Incorporating some basic footwork drills

Chapter 10

Focusing on Footwork

It's long been said that baseball is a game of inches. Well, boxing is a game of feet. Namely, where you place them in the ring and how you use them to advance, retreat, and create punching angles against your opponent.

It doesn't matter if you can run like Usain Bolt, moonwalk like Michael Jackson, and advance like General Patton on the beaches of Normandy. It all goes for naught if you can't get into position to land your punches. And that involves putting all those skills together in what is known, collectively, as *footwork*.

In many ways, footwork is the most essential of all boxing skills because the hardest puncher in the world will be completely ineffective if they can't get into position to land that punch. Footwork is also vital to an effective defense and sharp counterpunching. Knowing where to place your feet in the ring and in relation to your opponent is a subtle skill and it may not be the most exciting thing to work on, but mastering the art of maneuvering around a boxing ring and knowing how to move in, out, and side-to-side on an opponent will pay huge dividends when you decide to spar or fight.

The Old Soft-Shoe

Although we want to dig our toes into the canvas when punching to impart maximum power to our blows, it is essential that boxers be light on their feet when jockeying for position in the ring. That means maintaining the proper stance and spacing of your feet (slightly wider than shoulder width), keeping your knees slightly bent, and balancing lightly on the balls of your feet, as shown in Figure 10-1.

FIGURE 10-1: The proper foot position for balance and easy maneuverability in the ring.

with permission of Anthony Policano

Once again, your basic stance is profiled to your opponent with your nondominant leg and hand in front and your dominant leg and hand in the rear. This means that if you're right-handed, you should stand with your left leg forward and right leg back. (See Figure 10-2.) Southpaws do the reverse. You should balance on the ball of your rear foot with the heel slightly elevated. This allows for easy movement in any direction. (See Figure 10-3.)

FIGURE 10-2: Your front foot should be about 12 inches in front of your rear foot.

with permission of Anthony Policano

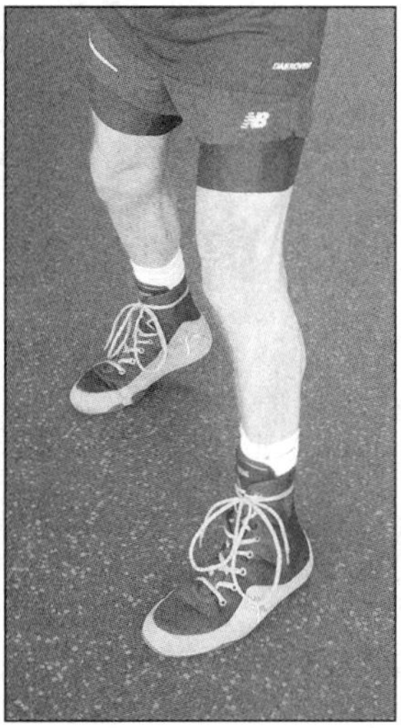

FIGURE 10-3: The heel of your rear foot should be slightly elevated to allow for easy movement in any direction.

with permission of Anthony Policano

No matter what you do or where you go in the ring, that stance should not change. You advance by taking a step forward with your front leg and following with your back leg. You retreat by taking a step back with your rear leg and following with your front leg. And you must always maintain the proper spacing and the profile posture toward your opponent. (This changes slightly if you have an opponent with their back against the ropes, however, in which case you would adjust your stance to be more square.)

Climb That Ladder

A very useful tool for honing your boxing footwork is a standard agility ladder. (See Figure 10-4.) Start with a basic drill: Lay the ladder in front of you horizontally and position yourself about a foot outside the first box. That would be the rightmost box if you are right-handed and jabbing with your left and the leftmost if you are a southpaw and jabbing with your right.

FIGURE 10-4: A basic agility ladder is useful for many footwork drills.

Courtesy of TITLE Boxing

Now, step in with your front foot while snapping out your jab. (See Figure 10-5.) Remember, the foot and fist should move together, and the fist should never be more than a few inches ahead of the foot, otherwise you'll throw your weight forward, leaving yourself off-balance and vulnerable.

Next, quickly draw back your foot and fist to the starting position and, with your front foot, take a step toward the next box. Repeat the step-and-jab move until you reach the end of the ladder, at which point you will pivot quickly on your front foot so that you now face in the opposite direction. (See Figure 10-6.) Continue the drill down the length of the ladder.

FIGURE 10-5: Practice your step-and-jab in each box of the agility ladder.

with permission of Anthony Policano

FIGURE 10-6: When you reach the last box, pivot quickly on your front foot and repeat the drill coming back.

with permission of Anthony Policano

Once you've got that one down, you can do the same drill, only now firing a one-two with the step. Progress to a one-two and hook and eventually to a one-two-hook-and-cross combo, remembering to pivot every time you reach the end of the ladder.

When it's time to pivot, you will do so on your front foot, turning either right or left in coordination with the movement of your opponent or trainer. (See Figures 10-7, 10-8, and 10-9.) As you pivot, your back foot repositions behind you, always maintaining the correct distance. We never want to bring our feet together or spread them too far apart; this will result in a critical loss of balance. This drill is best done on an agility ladder. Keep your front foot in the box and practice spinning on the ball of that foot so that you end up in your basic stance but facing in the opposite direction. This is a good method of reversing an opponent who has you in a corner or on the ropes.

FIGURE 10-7: Keep your front foot planted as you begin the pivot, turning to your right so you're still facing your opponent.

with permission of Anthony Policano

Incorporate this drill into every workout, perhaps immediately following your warmup, and you will soon find that your footwork has improved significantly.

Remember, you are dancing lightly on the balls of your feet, not standing flat-footed or plodding heavily on the canvas, but bouncing and gliding gracefully in the manner of a fencer or even a ballet dancer. One of the greatest of all heavyweight champions, Evander Holyfield, honed his footwork by taking lessons from Twyla Tharp, a preeminent ballet choreographer.

FIGURE 10-8: Quickly spin on the ball of your front foot.

with permission of Anthony Policano

FIGURE 10-9: Complete the pivot and return to your starting position, your basic fighting stance.

with permission of Anthony Policano

The best way to develop this skill is through rope skipping (discussed in Chapter 7) and shadowboxing, a portion of which should be devoted solely to moving fluidly around the ring or gym floor. Practice lightly skittering around the perimeter of the ring or workout surface with your hands up and your feet correctly positioned and spaced. Throw in a pivot or two in both directions, imagining that an opponent is moving in front of you. Try moving forward and backward. When you get comfortable with those basic moves, you can move on to more advanced techniques.

More Advanced Footwork Drills

Some more complex footwork drills can be performed with an agility cube (see Figure 10-10), which is similar to an agility ladder except that it is square and divided into 9 or 16 boxes. This allows you to work on advancing, retreating and sidestepping and pivoting while keeping the proper distance between your feet. If you don't have access to an agility cube, you can simulate one with tape on your gym floor.

FIGURE 10-10: An agility cube is a good tool for learning to advance, retreat, and sidestep while maintaining proper foot spacing.

Courtesy of TITLE Boxing

Controlling the space

Now that you've learned how to glide around the ring, it is time to take your footwork to the next level. That is determining where you want the fight to be fought, and insuring that it is fought there. Remember, the ring is your ballroom. Use every inch of it to your advantage.

For example, if you are a stick-and-move boxer à la Muhammad Ali or Sugar Ray Leonard, you will probably prefer the action to take place along the perimeter of the ring. That will require you to master the art of moving sideways around your opponent without getting trapped along the ropes. A useful drill is to practice sidestepping properly in the agility cube. Start by taking your normal boxing stance with your front foot in the front leftmost box and your rear foot in the box diagonally behind it. (See Figure 10-11.) If you are a left-handed boxer, start in the front rightmost box.

FIGURE 10-11: Start by taking your normal stance with your front foot in the front leftmost box and your rear foot in the box diagonally behind it.

with permission of Anthony Policano

If you want to stop your opponent from moving to the left, take a step sideways with your right foot, and then follow with your left, keeping your spacing correct at all times. (See Figures 10-12 and 10-13.)

FIGURE 10-12: When your opponent moves right, your first step is with your rear foot.

with permission of Anthony Policano

FIGURE 10-13: Follow with your front foot to keep your spacing and balance correct.

with permission of Anthony Policano

If you want to stop your opponent from moving to the right, step first with your left foot and follow with your right. (See Figure 10-14.)

FIGURE 10-14: When your opponent moves to your left, step first with your left foot.

with permission of Anthony Policano

When you are advancing on your opponent, the first step, obviously, is with the front foot, followed by the back foot. (See Figures 10-15 and 10-16.)

While advancing, your rear foot must follow so that your feet aren't spread too far apart, compromising your balance, as shown in Figure 10-16.

When using the agility cube, remember to be mindful of your foot position at all times. Never allow your feet to wind up in the same box (as in Figure 10-17), or to be in adjacent boxes, leaving you square to your opponent (as in Figure 10-18). Always keep your front foot and rear foot in boxes diagonal to each other. (See Figure 10-19.)

FIGURE 10-15: Step with your front foot when advancing on an opponent.

with permission of Anthony Policano

FIGURE 10-16: Your next step is with your rear foot, keeping the proper spacing and maintaining a profile to your opponent.

with permission of Anthony Policano

FIGURE 10-17: Important! Never allow your feet to cross in the ring. It will leave you off-balance and vulnerable.

with permission of Anthony Policano

FIGURE 10-18: Avoid landing with your feet in adjacent boxes, as this will leave you square to your opponent.

with permission of Anthony Policano

FIGURE 10-19: This is always how your feet should wind up after any maneuver.

with permission of Anthony Policano

Taking the proper stance

At the risk of repeating myself, let me emphasize that a boxer's foot position is vital for getting into position to land punches. When a right-handed boxer is fighting another right-handed boxer, the front (left) foot should be positioned between the two feet of the opponent. (See Figure 10-20.)

FIGURE 10-20: The proper foot position when a righty is fighting a righty.

with permission of Anthony Policano

This position makes it easier to slip the opponent's left jab with a move to the right, keeps the boxer safely outside his opponent's fists, and creates an angle to land a counterpunch. (See Figure 10-21.)

FIGURE 10-21: With your front foot between your opponent's feet, you can safely slip a left jab with a duck to the right.

with permission of Anthony Policano

When a right-handed boxer is fighting a southpaw (left-handed boxer), the front foot should be positioned to the outside of the opponent's front (right) foot. (See Figure 10-22.)

This makes it easier to slip the opponent's right jab with a duck to the left (see Figure 10-23) and facilitates a counterpunch to the body (see Figure 10-24) or head with a left hook.

Most boxers will find it more comfortable to move in the direction of their jabbing hand, meaning that right-handers will want to circle leftward and southpaws will want to circle to the right, behind their lead hands. But it is important to periodically mix it up and move back the other way, or else your movement will become predictable to your opponent, who will easily find a way to counter you.

Practice moving in both directions as part of your shadowboxing routine.

FIGURE 10-22: When a righty is fighting a lefty, this is where that front foot should be.

with permission of Anthony Policano

FIGURE 10-23: With your foot outside the opponent's front foot, you can safely slip a jab with a duck to the left.

with permission of Anthony Policano

FIGURE 10-24: Slipping to your left facilitates a counter hook to the body.

with permission of Anthony Policano

Keeping your distance

One of the most important and instinctual skills of a boxer is knowing how close — and at the same time, how far away — they must be to effectively land their punches without being in range of their opponent's shots. Your optimal distance from an opponent is the distance just close enough for you to land your jab (see Figure 10-25), a starting point from which you can easily step forward to land other punches if the opening arises, and just as easily step backward to avoid a counterpunch, or simply to reset yourself for another attack. Practice stepping in and out while jabbing, preferably with the use of an agility ladder.

Forward, march!

The most effective punches, of course, are landed while the fighter is moving forward. To do this effectively, you step forward with your front foot while punching and follow with your back foot, keeping the proper spacing so that you don't leave yourself off-balance. Practice advancing across the ring or your workout space one step and one jab at a time. When you reach the end, quickly pivot (make a 180-degree turn) on your front foot and repeat the advance in the opposite direction.

FIGURE 10-25: Use a torso bag or heavy bag to determine the proper distance for landing your jab effectively while being able to stay out of range of your opponent's counterpunches.

with permission of Anthony Policano

Taking a step back

There comes a time when even the most intrepid warrior must retreat. In boxing as in life, discretion is often the better part of valor. In those instances, the way to do this is by taking your first step with your back foot and following with your front foot, again maintaining the proper spacing for optimal balance. To this you should add some side-to-side movement of your head and upper body while keeping your hands up in a guarding position. Practice this the opposite way you practiced your advance. Start at one end of the ring or exercise floor and move backward, pivoting on your back foot when your back finds the ropes or the far wall.

Turn that ring into a phone booth

Back in the 1900s, before we were attached at the hand to these expensive devices known as smartphones, there were little glass boxes on city street corners in which people could make phone calls when outside the home. They were called phone booths and were barely big enough to dial the phone in, although Superman seemed to have no trouble changing clothes in them.

In any case, it's useful to know how to turn a 20-foot square boxing ring into an area the size of a phone booth, with a technique called cutting off the ring. The pursuing boxer (presumably you) moves in a specific pattern to force the opponent back to the ropes and, ideally, into a corner. It involves taking the proper steps with your feet to block an opponent's lateral movement and moving in diagonal lines rather than following your opponent around the ring. Joe Frazier, George Foreman, and Julio César Chávez were especially skilled at quickly turning the ring into a suffocatingly small space.

It's really not as complicated as it sounds. The simplest way to cut off the ring is merely to step sideways with your opponent. In other words, if the opponent is moving to the left, you will step first with your right foot. If the opponent is moving to the right, you will step first with your left. It's something like when two people come together on the sidewalk and while attempting to walk past each accidentally step into each other's way. Except in the ring, it's no accident. You want to get in the other boxer's way. They step left, you step right. They step right, you step left. In either case, you're advancing with your hands up, or better still, punching to the body, which is always a stationary target. Before you know it, the opponent has run out of room and you've got them where you want them, on the ropes or in a corner.

IN THIS CHAPTER

» How to avoid getting hit

» Learning to block punches

» Learning to slip punches

» How the greats did it

Chapter 11

Developing a Defense

Let's be honest here: In boxing, as in baseball, hitting is the most fun part of the game. But believe it or not, avoiding getting hit is probably the most important.

Not only is getting hit by punches extremely dangerous, it is also exhausting. Getting hit repeatedly not only damages you in the short-term and the long run, it also tires you out quickly and prevents you from landing your own punches. So it's essential that you learn the fine art of not getting hit. There are several ways to do this, and often the one you choose will be based on your body type and fighting style.

Blocking, Catching, and Parrying

This is the most basic form of boxing defense, and it simply involves using your gloves to block, deflect, or knock down your opponent's punches.

- **Blocking** a punch entails keeping your gloves high at all times and using your glove as a buffer between your opponent's fist and your face. It's the most rudimentary form of boxing defense and the one a beginning boxer should learn first. (See Figure 11-1.) The downside of using your glove to block a punch is that it temporarily takes that fist out of play, especially for beginners. You can't use it to counterpunch when it's busy blocking.

FIGURE 11-1: Blocking a punch with your gloves is the most rudimentary form of boxing defense.

with permission of Anthony Policano

- **Catching** a punch is slightly different in that the boxer uses an open glove to "catch" the opponent's punch, much in the way you would catch a baseball. (See Figure 11-2.) The boxer doing the catching can then knock down the incoming punch and deliver a counterpunch over it. This is a more advanced maneuver that will take plenty of practice and repetition.
- **Parrying** is a form of defense in which a boxer uses their glove to deflect an opponent's punch and redirect it either downward or to the outside, similar to brushing away a fly coming toward your face. It's most effective against straight punches, and it's the most effective way of both blocking a punch and creating an opening for a counterpunch. Parrying can be a chopping motion that knocks a punch down (see Figure 11-3) or a sideways motion (see Figure 11-4) that catches the inside of an opponent's punch and renders it harmless. Either way, it usually creates an opening for a straight counterpunch.

There is also a method of stopping an opponent's punch virtually before it starts, which is done by simply tapping the opponent on the bicep or shoulder as they begin a punch. You'll be surprised at how effective this slight movement is at deflecting blows.

FIGURE 11-2: Catching a punch with an open glove allows an experienced boxer to deliver a counterpunch.

with permission of Anthony Policano

FIGURE 11-3: Parrying a punch downward allows a boxer to counter over it.

with permission of Anthony Policano

FIGURE 11-4: Parrying to the side allows a boxer to counter inside the opponent's punch.

with permission of Anthony Policano

Slip Slidin' Away

Some boxers choose not to use their gloves for defense, preferring to make their opponents miss punches by moving their heads and upper bodies, thereby freeing their hands to deliver counterpunches. This is called *slipping punches*. Executed correctly, a proper slip will cause your opponent's punch to slide harmlessly over your shoulder (see Figure 11-5), leaving you safe and them exposed to your counter shots.

You can practice this tactic with a slip ball (see Figure 11-6), which is a baseball-sized leather bag hanging from a rope at about the height of your chin. You swing it back and forth and practice slipping it to both sides as it sails toward you.

Some of the greatest fighters in history have employed this method of defense, notably Jack Dempsey, Joe Frazier, Roberto Duran and Mike Tyson.

FIGURE 11-5: Slipping a punch is a simple but effective move, but it takes practice to master.

with permission of Anthony Policano

FIGURE 11-6: A slip ball is an effective device for learning how to bob and weave under punches.

Courtesy of TITLE Boxing

The Dempsey roll

This style involves slipping a punch, rolling underneath it, and then coming up with your own counter shot. This technique allowed the 6-foot-1 Jack Dempsey to get inside the arms of much taller heavyweights to land devastating head and body shots. Dempsey used it to great effect in his three-round destruction of 6-foot-6 Jess Willard to win the heavyweight title in 1919. He would do it by slipping to his right as his opponent jabbed, allowing the punch to pass harmlessly over his left shoulder. (See Figure 11-7.) Then, in the same motion, he would bend forward at the waist and rotate his upper body in a circular motion to the left, transferring his weight to his left leg. From there, his left hand would be loaded to deliver a powerful hook. The video of his first knockdown of Willard in their title fight is readily available on the Internet and should be studied by anyone planning to use this maneuver.

FIGURE 11-7: To execute the Dempsey roll, start by slipping to your right, continue the motion by bending forward and moving your body in a circular motion from right to left, then land a left hook.

with permission of Anthony Policano

After you've successfully completed the slip and roll, you'll be in a perfect position to land your hook to the body or head. (See Figures 11-8 and 11-9.)

FIGURE 11-8: After the roll, you can throw that hook to the body . . .

with permission of Anthony Policano

FIGURE 11-9: . . . or to the head.

with permission of Anthony Policano

The Frazier bob-and-weave

Smokin' Joe Frazier, the former heavyweight champion from Philadelphia who handed Muhammad Ali his first career defeat, was a perpetual motion machine whose head and upper body were in constant side-to-side movement. He employed more of a bob-and-weave style that involved both side-to-side and up-and-down movement of his torso. (See Figure 11-10.) He was an unpredictable target because his movement was fluid and constantly advancing. Unlike Dempsey, Frazier was able to slip punches from either hand and put himself into position to land counterpunches with both fists. Frazier's movement was largely instinctual and difficult to teach. It involves constant forward movement and close concentration on your opponent's fists. It also requires the kind of built-in natural radar that not many of us were born with. The former welterweight champion Wilfred Benítez was another boxer who had an uncanny ability to slip punches.

FIGURE 11-10: The Frazier bob-and-weave requires a built-in radar not many of us were born with!

United Press International, Inc. / Wikimedia Commons / Public domain

The Tyson Peek-a-boo

Mike Tyson's style of avoiding punches was similar to Dempsey's and Frazier's in that it was based on head movement rather than the use of gloves to block his opponent's punches. The difference was in his use of the so-called Peek-a-boo style in which the gloves were held up in front of the face, palms facing in, as he moved side-to-side in metronomic fashion. (See Figure 11-11.) This is an effective style of defense because it puts you in position to land with either hand — slip right, and you can land a right to the body; slip left, and you can hook to the body or head — but it can also become predictable if you're always moving in the same rhythm.

FIGURE 11-11: The Peek-a-boo defense as employed by Mike Tyson.

Mirrorpix/Getty Images

The Foreman/Norton crisscross, or "Mummy Defense"

Former champions George Foreman and Ken Norton (and to a lesser extent, Frazier) employed a novel defense in which their arms were crossed in front of their faces to absorb punches on their shoulders and biceps. (See Figure 11-12.) Neither one of them employed much head movement and this style often left them open to hooks and other looping punches. Of course, when you could punch like Foreman, who had one of the highest knockout percentages of any heavyweight champion in history, you can get away with it. For the rest of us mortals, I would suggest avoiding this style.

FIGURE 11-12: A George Foreman–type cross-arm defense.

with permission of Anthony Policano

The Ali shuffle and lean back

We all know the old saying, "He who fights and runs away lives to fight another day." Well, contrary to some opinions, Muhammad Ali never ran away from any opponent. But he did use his incredible footwork, leg speed, and reflexes to create an effective defense that was uniquely his own. The young Ali circled the perimeter of the ring, often changing direction, and his movement made it difficult if not impossible for most of his opponents to set their feet and punch. This style requires great cardio fitness — if you don't think so, just try skittering around the ring for 15 three-minute rounds without an opponent chasing you — and the kind of bounce in your legs that involves a lot of rope skipping and roadwork.

Another Ali defensive tactic was to lean straight back from punches, causing them to fall short of their target. (See Figure 11-13.) This is the opposite of what fighters like Frazier and Dempsey did; they moved forward while slipping side-to-side, thereby both causing opponents to miss and closing the distance to where they could land their own shots. Ali's tactic was effective for him, but not recommended for the rest of us. His supernatural reflexes allowed him to get away with this risky tactic, but for the average human being, pulling straight back will just put you right in line of an aggressive opponent's attack. In other words, don't do it.

FIGURE 11-13: Ali's incredible reflexes allowed him to lean back like this to avoid punches.

United Press International, Inc. / Wikimedia Commons / Public domain

Covering Up and Clinching

There will be times in any fight when the boxer will have no choice but to "cover up," which means pulling back into a protective shell to block an opponent's punches. The way to do this is to tuck your chin down tightly into your chest, pull your elbows in to the sides of your body, and hold your gloves up at about the level of your nose. (See Figure 11-14.) Even though your head is down, remember to keep your eyes open and peer upward at your opponent. Getting hit with a punch you don't see is among the worst things that can happen in the boxing ring.

FIGURE 11-14: Sometimes you just gotta cover up!

Focus On Sport/Getty Images

There also will be times when the wise move is simply to tie up your opponent's arms in a clinch. Excessive clinching is a foul and can result in a points deduction or, in extreme cases, disqualification. But every so often you will simply have to stop your opponent from punching to catch a breather. The way I do it is to thrust the glove of my front (left) hand into the crook of my opponent's right arm and lock my elbow so he can't move while simultaneously locking down his front glove in the crook of my right arm. (See Figure 11-15.) Then I hold until the referee comes in to break us.

FIGURE 11-15: You can lock down an opponent in a clinch like so.

with permission of Anthony Policano

IN THIS CHAPTER

» My typical boxing workout, from warmup to cooldown

» Bags, mitts, and sparring

» Core work, stretching, and cooling

Chapter 12
Running through a Typical Boxing Workout

This is the workout, with some variations to keep things interesting, that I put my students through five days a week. It incorporates everything from a comprehensive warmup, to between 10 and 12 rounds of shadowboxing, bag work, and mitt work, and finishes up with some dumbbell and core work before we cool down for the day. We work in ratios of three minutes of work with 30–45 seconds of rest in between rounds. The entire workout takes about an hour.

Starting with the Warmup

We begin by warming up our shoulders, which are going to get the most work of any body part in boxing training. Without getting bogged down in too much anatomical gobbledygook, understand that the shoulder joint is the only one in the human body that moves in three planes — front to back, side to side, and rotationally — and we must warm it up in all three directions before we start throwing serious punches. (See Figure 12-1.)

FIGURE 12-1: We start by limbering up our shoulders with light (two-to-four pound) dumbbells.

with permission of Anthony Policano

First, everyone grabs a pair of light dumbbells of between two and four pounds. We then bend slightly at the waist, hands at our sides, and swing our hands overhead in a steady, controlled motion similar to the motion of a jumping jack. We do that for 15–30 seconds before switching to letting our arms hang at our sides, palms facing backward, and raising and lowering our arms as if motioning someone to sit down. We do that for another 15–30 seconds. (See Figure 12-2.)

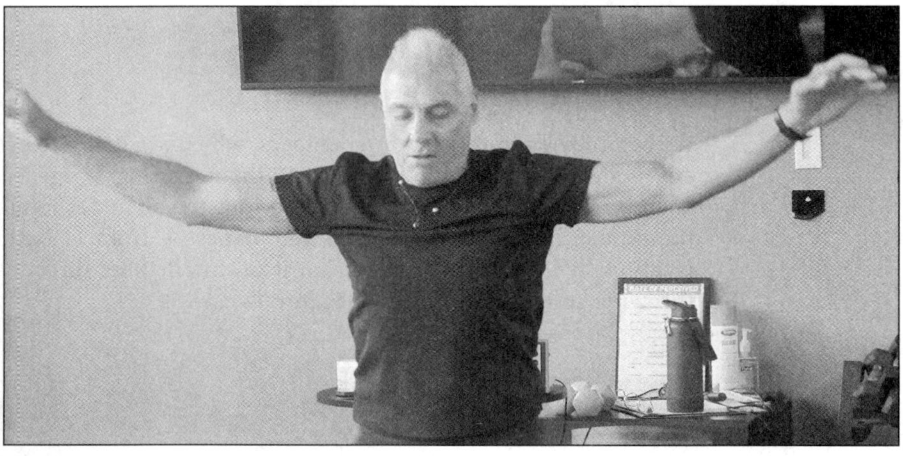

FIGURE 12-2: We activate the shoulder joint in all three planes of movement before we start punching.

with permission of Anthony Policano

Next, we extend our arms straight out from the shoulders and twirl them in small circles going forward. (See Figure 12-3.)

After a dozen or so of these, we make the same motion, only backward. Then we make the circles bigger, forward and then backward. These motions resemble freestyle and backstroke swimming strokes. We finish our shoulder warmup by performing a crossover stretch — one arm pulled straight across the chest while the other arm, in front and in a vertical position, lightly tugs on the deltoid muscle. We hold this for about 10 seconds and then switch arms.

FIGURE 12-3: I demonstrate the combinations to throw in the workout.

with permission of Anthony Policano

Then, still holding the dumbbells, we shadowbox lightly for 30 seconds, throwing punches easily, turning our hips on each punch, concentrating on correct form and aiming for fluidity of movement. At this point I generally move around the room, explaining what combinations we will be throwing in the workout and correcting form errors.

Occasionally at this point we jump rope for one three-minute round, but quite frankly, when I have a full class (12 or more), it becomes chaotic and borderline dangerous to have a dozen people swinging leather ropes, so we often skip it (no pun intended). But if you're training alone or in a gym with enough room for everyone, I suggest a round or two of rope jumping at this juncture of the warmup to limber up your legs.

If you aren't yet adept at rope skipping or don't have a big enough room or high enough ceiling to jump comfortably, you can do a couple of simple agility ladder drills. First, run through the agility ladder, placing one foot in each box while lifting the knees high (see Figures 12-4 and 12-5).

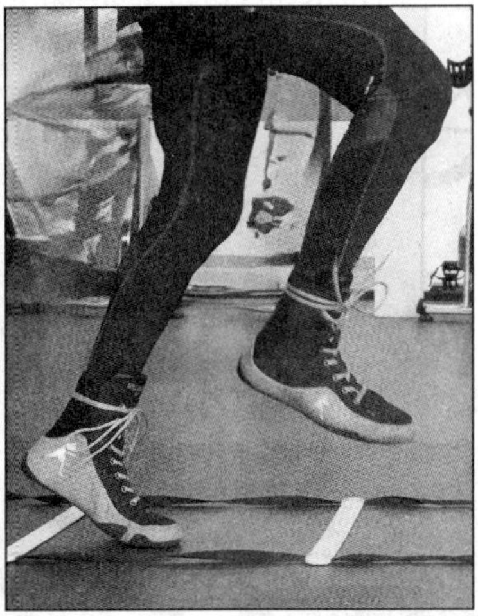

FIGURE 12-4: Run through the agility ladder placing one foot in each box while high-stepping all the way.

with permission of Anthony Policano

FIGURE 12-5: Remember, keep those knees high all the way through.

with permission of Anthony Policano

We run through the ladder that way five times, and then switch to a choppy step, placing two feet in each box (see Figure 12-6). We do that five times and we're warmed up and ready to proceed to the fun stuff!

FIGURE 12-6: It's a little tougher to run the agility ladder while placing both feet in each box with short, choppy steps.

with permission of Anthony Policano

Moving On to Shadowboxing

Now that our shoulders are loose and we have a good sweat going, I switch on the gym timer and we shadowbox for one three-minute round. "Shadowboxing" has nothing to do with shadows, of course. It is essentially fake boxing against an invisible opponent during which we practice our basic movements, starting from the ground up. Ideally, shadowboxing should be done in a ring, and always performed within sight of a mirror so you can monitor your form and balance and correct any mistakes, such as dropping your hands (see Figure 12-7). You can shadowbox without a mirror, of course, but you will find it difficult to know when you are doing something incorrectly. It's a lot easier to correct our mistakes when we can see them for ourselves rather than having someone else point them out. But even if you have no access to a ring or mirror, shadowboxing should be a staple of the early portion of your workout.

When you shadowbox, you should concentrate on form over speed, and imagine you are facing an opponent. Work on all your punches: your jab, your double jab, your one-two, and any other combination you can think of. Always strive for proper technique and be mindful of getting your hands back into your starting position — fists up, chin down, and eyes on your imaginary foe.

with permission of Anthony Policano

FIGURE 12-7: Shadowboxing is best performed in front of a mirror to check your form and correct mistakes.

In my class, I begin by encouraging everyone just to bounce in place for a few seconds, and then to glide around the workout floor, imagining they just climbed into the ring and are moving around the surface to get the feel of the canvas. Then I run through what our combination sequence will be for that workout. I move from student to student, demonstrating how the combinations should be thrown and correcting errors of form and technique.

In shadowboxing, bag work, and mitt work (see Figure 12-8), we work three-minute rounds divided into 30-second chunks, meaning that every 30 seconds a bell rings, prompting the class to switch to the next combination.

A typical basic sequence for beginners might look like this:

1. **0–30 seconds: Jabs**
2. **30–60 seconds: One-two (jab and cross)**
3. **60–90 seconds: One-two-three (jab, cross, and hook)**
4. **90–120 seconds: One-two-three-two (jab, cross, hook, cross)**
5. **120–150 seconds: One-two-three-two-three (jab, cross, hook, cross, hook)**
6. **150 seconds–bell: Two-four-six-eight-ten (A drill in which the boxer throws two punches, then four, then six, then eight, then ten, and repeats the sequence until the bell — designed to bring on exhaustion!)**

FIGURE 12-8: A good mitt workout is as close to a sparring session without getting hit.

with permission of Anthony Policano

TIP

The reason we conclude each round with the strenuous two-four-six-eight-ten drill is because fight judges tend to remember the last thing they see when scoring a round, and putting on a strong closing flurry is a good way to "steal" a close round. And even if you never plan to step into a boxing ring, it is always a good idea to finish up strong in all your workouts.

With an intermediate or advanced group, I generally change up the routine as follows:

1. **0–30 seconds: One-twos**
2. **30–60 seconds: Jab, uppercut, and hook**
3. **60–90 seconds: Jab-cross-hook-uppercut**
4. **90–120 seconds: Jab-cross-slip-and-roll and hook**
5. **120–150 seconds: Jab-cross-hook-uppercut-hook-cross**
6. **150–bell: Two-four-six-eight-ten**

Most days, we repeat the same sequence for every round of the workout. If it seems like drudgery, remember that in boxing, repetition makes perfect. Practicing the same punching patterns over and over again helps them become second nature so the boxer can execute them without having to think about them in the heat of battle.

Graduating to Bag Punching

The above sequence is executed by the students on the array of bags in my gym. That includes a rack of heavy bags, a torso bag, a cobra bag, and a double-end bag. The heavy bag rack includes both conventional bags, filled with a dense, resistant fabric-like material, and softer, more forgiving water-filled bags. We also utilize two uppercut bags, which are similar to heavy bags but mounted horizontally to allow easier access for punches thrown from underneath.

The way I work it is that each student gets to perform the sequence with me on the punch mitts, which affords an opportunity for individualized instruction (and often results in an intense workout, because everyone wants to impress the instructor!). The remaining students rotate from bag to bag each round, so everyone gets to work on a variety of bags and punching surfaces (see Figure 12-9). We work in ratios of three minutes of work to 30 seconds of rest. It's a tough workout, but, frankly, when I've increased the rest period to a minute or even 45 seconds, my students complain that's too long!

FIGURE 12-9: All the bags are in use as the group goes through its workout routine.

with permission of Anthony Policano

If you're not part of a boxing class or you prefer to work alone, I suggest the following workout:

1. **A warmup sequence such as that described above, with or without light dumbbells**
2. **Two three-minute rounds of shadowboxing, preferably before a mirror**
3. **Two three-minute rounds of rope skipping**
4. **Two three-minute rounds apiece on the speed bag, the double-end bag, the cobra bag, and the heavy bag, for a total of 12 rounds of work (If you don't have access to all the specialty bags, do four rounds apiece on the speed and heavy bags.)**
5. **A strength and core workout similar to the ones described later in this chapter**
6. **A cooldown**

Adding Sparring to the Mix

Since the vast majority of my students have no real aspirations to become boxers but are just looking for an intense and effective workout, we don't spar in my classes. But if you're serious about wanting to box competitively, sparring regularly is a must. It's the only way to find out several important things about your skills and yourself.

For one thing, you discover whether what you've been practicing so hard on the bags and mitts actually works against a real person, and if not, it's your job to figure out how to remedy that. What you're likely to learn is that it's difficult to get into the proper position to land solidly against a moving target, a problem you did not encounter against the bags or mitts. That's where footwork and defensive ability play a huge role, two topics we cover in Chapters 10 and 11.

TIP

There's an old saying that everything is a lot harder when the other guy is trying, and you'll find that it's much more difficult to land effective blows on a moving target that's hitting back. Don't be discouraged by this. Just know that it will happen to you the first few times you spar.

For another, the first time you get hit by another boxer, you'll quickly learn whether boxing really is for you. You know that old quip, "It's all fun and games until someone loses an eye"? Well, boxing is a blast until someone gets clocked. A lot of very tough people get hit hard for the first time and decide "This is not for me." And that's fine. The first time I got into the ring with a real boxer, I frankly was shocked by how fast, snappy, and powerful the punches were. This was not the game I had been playing with my friends. But I discovered that not only could I withstand the impacts, but I kind of enjoyed the give-and-take. Still, I resolved to land more and get hit less — always a wise policy. Your reaction to your first experience with real punching will determine whether you'll use boxing as a workout or pursue it as a competition.

If you do decide to spar (and if your gym offers it), do it after your warmup and before any strenuous bag work, when your energy and strength are at their peak.

REMEMBER

You should always approach sparring as a learning experience, not a simulated fight. Think of it like batting practice, where you work on certain things, especially those you are weakest in. That is why you should always choose a sparring partner who has the same mindset and isn't trying to hurt you or prove something. It should be a session in which both of you are working on techniques and fundamentals. That doesn't mean you should "pull your punches" — that is, punch with less power than you normally would — but it does mean you should moderate the intensity of your attack and concentrate on improving your skills rather than on fattening your record.

My Numbering System

I use a simple numbering system to let my clients know what punches I want them to throw:

- **One** is a jab.
- **Two** is a cross.
- **Three** is a hook to the head.
- **Four** is an uppercut to the head thrown with the rear hand.
- **Five** is a shovel hook to the body thrown with the front hand.
- **Six** is a punch to the body thrown with the rear hand delivered at a 45-degree angle upward similar to the shovel hook.

That's it. With those six punches we can throw a limitless number of combinations, such as these:

- **One-two:** A simple jab and cross, the most basic of boxing combos
- **One-two-three:** A jab, cross, and hook
- **One-two-three-two:** A jab, cross, hook, and cross
- **One-two-three-four:** Jab, cross, hook, and uppercut, all to the head
- **One-four-three-two:** Jab, uppercut, hook, and cross, all to the head
- **One-two-five:** A jab and cross to the head, followed by a hook to the body
- **Four-two-three:** A hook to the body followed by a cross and hook to the head
- **Five-six-three-two:** Body shots with the front and rear hands, followed by a hook and cross to the head

We also include defensive variations, such as the *slip and counter*, in which the trainer jabs at the boxer, who slips the punch over the front shoulder and fires back with a cross, and the *slip and roll*, in which the trainer jabs at the boxer, who slips the punch and then rolls underneath it, putting themselves in position to land with a hook. We also incorporate a "shoeshine and coverup" drill in which the boxer throws four body punches at the coach's hand pads and then rapidly covers up, pulling the elbows in, the gloves up and the chin down as the coach fires back with a couple of slaps to the elbows. It is designed to prepare the boxer to go quickly into a defensive shell when under attack.

As you can see, the possibilities of what you can do with those six basic punches are endless. Experiment with your own variations to avoid becoming predictable in your attack.

Strength Training

We don't do a lot of heavy-duty strength training because, as I note elsewhere, punching power is more a matter of technique than muscle. However, you need a fair amount of strength in the ring in order to avoid being shoved around and to control your opponent in the clinches.

Going old-school with dumbbells and weighted balls

After our bag work, we grab the weighted balls (anywhere from 6 to 12 pounds), lie on our backs, and perform two sets of 25 ball tosses. We start with the ball at the chest and thrust it as hard and powerfully as we can toward the ceiling. I warn my students to catch it, soft-handedly, before it hits the chest on the way down or you'll feel the way Jim Corbett did after being hit with the Solar Plexus Punch (refer to Chapter 9). The object of this exercise is to build explosiveness in our shoulders to increase speed and punching power.

Then we all grab a pair of dumbbells (ranging from 5 to 15 pounds, depending on the size and strength of the individual) to perform two sets of a four-count exercise I use to strengthen the triceps, biceps, and shoulders:

1. **Count 1:** We raise the dumbbells back behind us, turning our palms up to the ceiling to flex the triceps. (See Figure 12-10.)
2. **Count 2:** We swing them up to shoulder level, palms facing each other. This hits the biceps. (See Figure 12-11.)
3. **Counts 3 and 4:** We press the dumbbells twice overhead, turning our hands so that at the top of the movement, our palms are facing forward. This is a great shoulder strengthener. (See Figure 12-12.)

FIGURE 12-10: We start by kicking the dumbbells back and turning our palms toward the ceiling to hit the triceps.

with permission of Anthony Policano

We do 12 reps, rest for 30 seconds, and repeat with another set of 12.

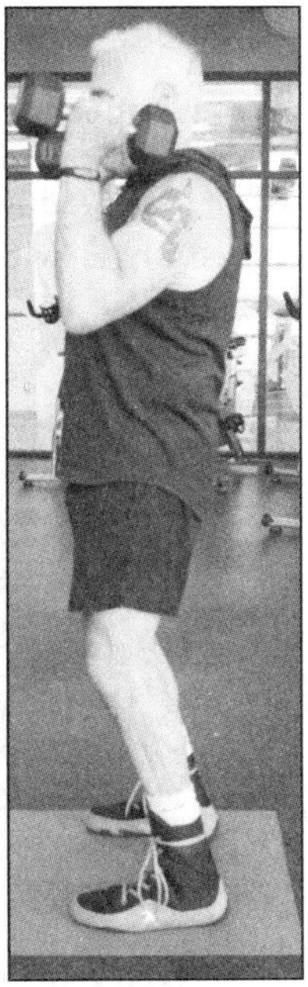

FIGURE 12-11: Next, we bring the dumbbells to our shoulders.

with permission of Anthony Policano

FIGURE 12-12: Finally, we press them overhead twice in rapid succession.

with permission of Anthony Policano

Another dumbbell workout we use is a combination of pushups and squats. We start by doing 10 pushups while leaning on a pair of dumbbells (see Figure 12-13), which allows us to go a little deeper on the way down. After the 10 pushups, we immediately come to our feet, holding the dumbbells at our shoulders, and squat, keeping our backs straight, achieving a 90-degree angle with our quads, and being careful to keep our feet pointing straight ahead.

FIGURE 12-13: Pushups on a pair of dumbbells allow us to go deeper than we would flat on the floor.

with permission of Anthony Policano

As we explode upward out of the squat, we press the dumbbells overhead. (See Figures 12-14, 12-15, and 12-16.)

We started out doing one set of 10 pushups and 10 squats, followed by sets of 15 and 15 and 20 and 20. But after a couple of weeks, we were able to increase to three sets of 20 and 20, and no doubt will eventually increase that, too.

FIGURE 12-14: Starting position for the squat.

with permission of Anthony Policano

FIGURE 12-15: Aim to get your thighs as close to parallel to the floor as you can.

with permission of Anthony Policano

FIGURE 12-16: Finish the movement by exploding out of the squat and raising the dumbbells overhead.

with permission of Anthony Policano

I suggest starting with the dumbbells slightly wider than shoulder-width on the first set of pushups, and move them a little closer on each successive set, so that by the third set they're nearly touching each other. This will ensure the exercise hits your shoulders, your chest, and your triceps.

Focusing on your core

A strong core is essential to punching power, as well as for overall physical conditioning, since all our power comes from our ability to rotate our hips. At the end of our workout, we sometimes perform two sets of Russian twists, performed sitting down with the knees and feet off the ground and the upper body at a 45-degree angle. We grasp a weight ball in both hands and twist rapidly from side to side, strengthening our obliques and abdominal wall.

Then we turn over onto all fours and perform a two-minute plank, in four 30-second segments — first, a flat plank, on hands or elbows, then 30 seconds each of a side plank, first one side, then the other. We go back to a flat plank for the last 30 seconds, and ideally add some mountain climbers, a modified running motion while in the plank position, to the mix. (See Figure 12-17.) It's basically balancing on your hands while you run in place while remembering to keep your abs braced and your glutes tight.

FIGURE 12-17: Mountain climbers are essentially running in place while planking.

with permission of Anthony Policano

TIP

"Abdominal bracing" is a technique in which the muscles of the midsection and back are tightened as if preparing to be hit by a punch in the stomach. It differs from pulling in your gut in that you can still breathe normally while doing it, and once you get the hang of it, you will find yourself doing it throughout your workout. Bracing stabilizes your core and does wonders for the strength of your *rectus abdominis* — the much coveted "six-pack." You will be surprised at how beneficial such a simple exercise can be.

During the plank stage, it really doesn't matter if you plank on your hands or on your elbows and forearms (see Figures 12-18 and 12-19). I prefer to plank on my elbows because my wrists are always sore from catching punches with the mitts. Whichever way you do it, the key to an effective plank is to keep your back flat, your abdomen braced, and your glutes tight throughout the movement.

FIGURE 12-18: Whether you plank on your hands or your elbows, it's important to keep your back flat and your core braced.

with permission of Anthony Policano

FIGURE 12-19: Planking on your hands can be tough on your wrists and shoulders.

with permission of Anthony Policano

Stretching and cooldown

Now comes everyone's favorite part of the workout. At the conclusion of the plank, I have everyone drop to their knees into what in yoga is called the *child's pose*:

hands and arms outstretched and the head to the floor, stretching the lower back, the shoulders, and the quads. (It's best to do this on a yoga mat.) We do it long enough for breathing to return to close to normal, generally between 30 and 60 seconds, and then roll over to do a full-body stretch, which is simply extending your arms, palms up, as far overhead as you can. Hold that position for 30 seconds, and then alternate stretching each arm further for an additional five seconds.

We then roll over onto all fours and come to our feet. We bend over at the waist and allow our shoulders to dangle, rotating them in gentle circles, for 30 seconds or so. Then we straighten up and repeat the shoulder warmup we did at the beginning of the workout, and finish up with a light "shakeout," which is a repeat of the hands-open punches we threw earlier.

We finish up with a deep cleansing breath and say bye-bye until the next one.

IN THIS CHAPTER

» Taking it to the next level

» Choosing the right gym

» Finding the right trainer

» Training like a pro

» Thinking like a fighter

» What to do on the day of the fight

» The bell rings: Now what?

Chapter 13 Preparing for the Big Day

OK, so you've been training in your basement or at a local health club for a while now and feel like you need a little more. You've gotten into better shape and learned a lot about boxing, but you want to see if all those techniques you've been working on against stationary objects actually work against an opponent who is not only moving but hitting back.

Well then, it's time to graduate to a real boxing gym, with real boxing trainers and serious boxers. So where do you start?

Finding a Gym

A good place to begin is at the USA Boxing website (`https://usaboxing.webpoint.us`), which maintains a database of more than 2,000 approved boxing gyms across the country. California and Texas each have over 300 boxing gyms and New York has approximately 150. Just go to their website, click on your state, enter your zip code, and you'll get a list of gyms in your area.

But how do you know that the gym you've chosen is the right one for you?

Well, every gym has a vibe, and if the vibe doesn't feel right to you, then the gym probably isn't. A boxing gym should be no different from any other health club, whether it's a Pilates studio, a yoga ashram, or a large fitness chain. The staff should be welcoming and the clientele at least somewhat supportive of new people. This is not always the case in hardcore boxing gyms, where competition runs high. Seek out a place where newcomers are taught carefully and brought along slowly. Avoid places that will throw a new boxer into the ring with someone more experienced or not likely to work constructively with a relatively inexperienced fighter.

General rule of thumb: If the management is willing to let a new boxer spar, sight unseen, on their first day in the gym, get out fast. Clearly, safety is not a priority there. Same rule applies if whoever is running the gym allows better, more experienced fighters to beat up on newbies or, worse yet, encourages young fighters to hurt one another in the ring. Remember, sparring is supposed to be a learning experience, not a fight. If the gym doesn't use sparring sessions as teaching moments for young fighters, it is not the right place for you.

And let's not lose track of the simple truth about actual boxing: It can be extremely dangerous. So be sure that the gym you choose recognizes and respects your skill and experience level and matches you accordingly.

Choosing a Trainer

Many smaller gyms have one or two trainers who work with every fighter. Larger places, such as Gleason's Gym in Brooklyn, New York, have a roster of trainers who can be hired for a fee. In just about every case, you're going to have to pay someone to train you, just as you would with any personal trainer in any health facility.

And choosing a boxing trainer is just like choosing a strength trainer. Each has a specialty and a specific way of training that may or may not mesh with your style of boxing. The qualities you should look for in a boxing trainer include knowledge, of course, but also flexibility and, believe it or not, honesty.

First off, you want a trainer who knows the techniques of boxing inside and out, and can teach them on both a physical and an intellectual level. Showing a boxer how to do something correctly is important, but so is explaining the reason why certain things are done. Some of us are visual learners and others need an explanation. I have found that a combination of both techniques works best. If I can make a student understand why a punch needs to be thrown a certain way, it's often easier for them to grasp the technique. Find someone whose approach incorporates both aspects.

Second, you want a trainer who is willing to work with your physical and mental attributes, not someone who wants to mold you into their idea of a boxer. Sad to say, some trainers insist on teaching all their boxers the same way without taking into account body type, athleticism, or temperament. Simply put, you can't take a Rocky Marciano-type heavyweight and try to turn him into Muhammad Ali, any more than you could take Ali and ask him to fight like Mike Tyson. A good trainer sizes up a boxer's strengths, weaknesses, and capabilities and tailors the approach accordingly.

Finally, you need a trainer who will be honest with you, and sometimes brutally so. Again, boxing can be extremely dangerous — there have been more than 1,300 recorded deaths in the boxing ring since the adoption of the Marquis of Queensbury Rules in 1884, and countless cases of *pugilistica dementia*, or "punch-drunk syndrome." Ali, one of the greatest boxers of all time, was rendered virtually speechless and immobile by Parkinson's syndrome, likely brought on by blows to the head. If it can happen to as gifted a fighter as Ali, it can happen to anybody. So it's important that you choose a trainer who will not only look out for your safety, but will let you know when it's time to quit — or even to let you know right off the bat that real boxing is not for you and that you're better off sticking to bag work. It may hurt to hear it, but it may also save your life. It takes compassion for a trainer to tell a boxer to hang it up. Find one who will tell you the truth.

Training Like a Pro

If you're really planning to fight, then training has to become almost a religion in the weeks leading up to the bout. That means running and putting in your gym time every day, watching your diet (including alcohol consumption), and getting the proper amount of sleep. It means temporarily doing without things you normally enjoy, such as partying or overindulging in food or drink, and it might mean having to pass on events with family or friends if it interferes with your training. There is a lot of sacrifice involved in serious boxing, and believe me, any corners you cut in the weeks leading up to a bout will come back to haunt you on fight night. Unlike other sports, a boxing match doesn't only take place on the day of the fight. It's a weeks-long process of preparation and conditioning, both physical and mental. If you're not prepared to commit to that, you're probably better off not fighting.

Developing a Fighter's Mindset

What exactly does that mean? It means believing in yourself at all costs. It means never assuming that anyone is better than you, regardless of appearance, reputation, or experience level. It means walking into the arena on fight night believing you can beat anyone in the building.

Of course, it's absolutely normal to be nervous, unsure, or even a little afraid. Every fighter who has ever stepped into a ring has experienced every one of those feelings before and even during a fight. But the mindset of a fighter has to be that they will overcome those feelings and win the fight.

Things to remember: Everything that you're feeling, your opponent is feeling, too. No matter how muscular or strong your opponent looks to you, they're made of the same raw material you are, and they feel the same pain and exhaustion. It's fine to feel nervous or apprehensive or even frightened. The important thing is not to show those things to your opponent. Let them think that you're the stronger, braver, tougher one in that ring. Remember: In boxing, as in life, it's not how you feel. It's what you show.

And one more thing: If you're properly trained and prepared for the bout, the odds are you'll perform well. Always remember this: If you do what you are capable of doing, it doesn't matter what your opponent does. You will win. To paraphrase JFK's famous inaugural address, think not of what your opponent can do to you. Think of what you're going to do to your opponent.

The Day of the Fight

Yes, you'll be nervous the day of the fight. Yes, you'll be antsy. You'll be torn by two emotions: not being able to wait for the fight to start, and not being able to imagine yourself actually fighting. Both are perfectly normal.

Your ideal fight day routine is one that you'll figure out the more often you fight, but a general rule of thumb is to try to approach it as a normal day with something important — and exciting — to be done that evening.

That means taking it easy most of the day without straying too far from your routine. It means going to work as normal, if your job is not physically demanding. It means eating what you normally would on an average day, but not eating any closer than about four hours before fight time. You want to feel light and energetic, not heavy and sluggish. It means no strenuous exercise during the day except for shaking out your arms and legs periodically to stay loose. You might want to do some light stretching or yoga, or even meditate for a bit to clear your mind.

When you get to the arena, you might want to wander out to the ring to get an idea of where you'll be working, and what it will feel like in front of the crowd. If you're fighting later — when I fought in the 1977 Golden Gloves, I was in the 24th bout of the night, which gave me plenty of time to relax, warm up, and relax again, several times over — you might want to peek at some of the earlier bouts. About 10 minutes before you enter the ring, you'll want to shadowbox lightly to warm up and break a sweat. You never want to go into a fight cold. And it's a good idea to go over a mental checklist in your mind, just to remind you of little things ("Remember to jab. Keep your chin tucked in") and bigger things ("This guy is supposed to have a good left hook. Keep that right hand up").

Most importantly, stay calm and focused because a loss of emotional control leads to disaster in the boxing ring. You need to observe your opponent closely and calmly, almost as if you were watching from ringside, in order to formulate your fight strategy and react to their movements.

The Bell Rings. Now What?

Now is when you put to work all those techniques you learned, all the conditioning you put yourself through, and all the analytical skills that your boxing brain has absorbed. Remember, as a boxer, you're a problem-solver, and you have an answer for anything your opponent does in that ring. Keep your eyes open and your mind relaxed but ready.

Understand that even in a so-called "easy" fight, you may get tired or hurt or feel discouraged. Allow me to repeat myself, because it bears repeating: Everything you're feeling, your opponent is feeling, too. Keep your wits about you and believe in your skills and the preparation that has brought you here.

Stay calm, stay focused, and stay tough. Those are the qualities that give you the best chance to win.

Nevertheless, be sure to keep the following points in mind:

- **Fighting is not sparring.** Even if you have been sparring a lot, expect a significant increase in intensity in an actual fight. Sparring is a learning experience. Fighting is a survival exercise. Remember, a boxing match is not a game and your opponent will not be playing. Although you may not have to, you must be prepared to fight intensely from the opening bell, and you must go in assuming your opponent will do the same. It's a lot better to be pleasantly surprised than unpleasantly shocked.

» **You are going to get hit.** Unless you were blessed with the defensive skills of Wilfred Benítez or Floyd Mayweather Jr., it's nearly impossible to get through a fight without getting hit at least once. Prepare yourself mentally for this reality and you'll be surprised at your tolerance for it. Believe me, we all react the same way when we accidentally bump into a door, but in the ring it's possible to achieve a pain threshold you would never display in real life. The important things are not to panic when you do get hit and not to get angry and lash out wildly in an attempt at immediate retaliation. A better use of your time and abilities is to think about why you got hit with that particular punch and formulate a strategy not to get hit by it again.

» **You will be nervous.** As I mentioned above, fight-time jitters are perfectly normal. After all, you're going into an endeavor that is extremely demanding, both mentally and physically. The better your preparation has been — both your physical training and your psychological conditioning — the less nervous you are likely to be, but the reality is that no matter how well your training went, the fight is still ahead of you. It's the same feeling you probably got before any big test in your life. You got through them and you'll get through this one.

» **You're likely to get exhausted at some point.** New boxers are especially prone to fatiguing early in fights for several reasons, the biggest being an excess of nervous energy that causes them to start too quickly or to fight frantically. It's difficult for inexperienced boxers to relax in the ring, but this will come the more sparring and fighting you do. But unless your fight ends in the first minute (with, hopefully, your hand raised in victory), every boxer will experience some form of exhaustion over the course of a bout. This is where proper techniques honed in the gym come into play. When you get tired in the ring, the thing to do is to take yourself out of the battle for a moment. That means stepping back, always with your hands up in your guarding position — there are no timeouts in boxing, and your opponent will not stop fighting because you need a rest — and take a deep breath or two before returning to action. Remember, only fools rush in. Boxers assess the situation in front of them and respond accordingly.

» **You might get confused in there.** Again, perfectly normal, especially for inexperienced boxers. I'll never forget my first time sparring in a ring, against a real fighter — he had been a Golden Gloves champion the year before — and how the entire experience seemed surreal and impossible to decode. Everything seemed to be happening too fast; his gloves were a red blur while mine seemed to be too heavy and too big, one constantly getting in the way of the other. But after a few sessions, everything seemed to slow down. I was able to see what the other boxer was doing, or trying to do. I suddenly discovered openings where before there was only chaos. I found that when I let my punches go, they landed, and when they landed, they had a visible effect. Once again, that was a result of relaxation in the ring, which only comes with experience and repetition. And, oh yeah, keep your eyes open at all times. It's only natural for human beings to blink or even close their eyes when something dangerous is coming toward their faces, but in boxing, this is disastrous. The punch you don't see is the one that will knock you out every time.

- **In spite of it all, you have a great chance to win.** Every one of the feelings you experience in a boxing match or a sparring session is being felt by your opponent, too. Nobody in boxing or in life is a Superman or Superwoman. We're all made of the same raw material, we all feel the same pain, and we all experience the same emotions. There is no shame in experiencing any of these things during the course of a bout, and after the fight is over, no one is going to know what was going through your mind anyway. All they will know is what you show them in the ring and, if you've been training diligently, what you show them will be admirable.
- **There is no better feeling than having your hand raised in victory, especially after a tough battle.** That's why, unlike in other sports where hostility sometimes lingers between teams and players after the game has ended, you often see boxers hugging one another after the final bell. There is a mutual respect that comes with battling another human being at close quarters, and it's rare that boxers show anger or dislike toward an opponent after a fight.

After all, they know what goes into preparing for a boxing match and what is asked of a boxer during a fight.

And if you decide to take your boxing to this level, you will, too.

5

Know the Players, Know the Game

IN THIS PART . . .

Find the best publications and websites to read about boxing and keep up with current happenings.

Score the fights like an expert.

Understand how fights are made, where the money comes from, and the responsibilities of promoters, matchmakers, managers, and trainers.

Learn the history and significance of amateur boxing, and how it differs from the professional sport.

IN THIS CHAPTER

- » How and where to watch and read about boxing
- » Learning to know what you're watching
- » Understanding how fights are scored
- » Knowing the rules
- » Learning the lingo

Chapter 14

Becoming the Perfect Fan

Although boxing training is more popular than ever these days, it seems as if it's harder to be a well-informed boxing fan than it ever was. Back in the day, major boxing matches were readily available on network television (for free!), every major newspaper sports section had a reporter who specifically and often exclusively covered boxing, and a multitude of magazines were devoted solely to the coverage of the fight game.

But now boxing coverage lives mostly on the Internet and, while televised boxing still exists, it's no longer on the networks and often comes with a hefty price tag.

Still, there are ways for boxing fans to get the scoop on their favorite sport.

Reading the Fights

For much of the first half of the 20th century, boxing was front-page news on just about every major newspaper in the US. The headline for the 1921 bout between Jack Dempsey and Georges Carpentier, the first boxing match to earn $1 million at the gate, was spread across the top of the entire front page of *The New York Times* (see Figure 14-1), and a half-century later, the *Times* gave similar coverage to the first bout between Muhammad Ali and Joe Frazier.

Section 1 | "All the News That's Fit to Print" | The New York Times. | THE WEATHER | Section 1

NEW YORK, SUNDAY, JULY 3, 1921. | FIVE CENTS

DEMPSEY KNOCKS OUT CARPENTIER IN THE FOURTH ROUND;
CHALLENGER BREAKS HIS THUMB AGAINST CHAMPION'S JAW;
RECORD CROWD OF 90,000 ORDERLY AND WELL HANDLED

HARDING ENDS WAR; SIGNS PEACE DECREE AT SENATOR'S HOME

Thirty Persons Witness Momentous Act in Frelinghuysen Living Room at Raritan.

...OPS BLOT ON SIGNATURE

Joint Resolution of Congress Made Effective at 4:10 P. M., Daylight Saving Time.

TEXT OF THE RESOLUTION

President Harding Asks, 'Was It a Good Fight?'

WIFE AND MOTHER BOTH TAKE POISON

Women Go to Hotel Commodore, Swallow Mercury, and Elder One Phones Physician.

FOUND CLASPING BABY SHOE

Young Woman Was Worried Because Husband Took Child to His Mother—Both May Die.

CROWD EARLY AT GATES

Thousands Wait Through Morning Hours for Opening of Arena

POLICE IN PERFECT CONTROL

Handle Entrance and Exit of Huge Throng Without Difficulty—1,000 Firemen on Guard.

CHEER NOTABLES IN ENTRY

Spectators Eat Lunches in Streets—Bootleggers and Crooks Noticeably Absent.

Dempsey's First Thought Is Telegram to His Mother

REFORMERS DEMAND ARREST OF DEMPSEY

and They Fail to Get Plea Before Any Judge.

NEW MOVE EXPECTED TODAY

Assault and Battery Charged in Complaint—Not So "Brutal" as They Anticipated.

COBB FIGHTS IT OVER AGAIN

Calls Carpentier Soul of the Fray, Dempsey the Body.

ALL WHO'S BALLYHOO THERE

Arts, Science, Drama, Politics, Bar, Bench and Commerce Are Represented.

BOYLE'S 30 ACRES FERTILE

If There Is No New War, He Thinks Jack Will Be Best Fighter for a While.

Dempsey Says He Won Just as He Thought He Would; Carpentier Asserts He Staked His All in the Second

CARPENTIER BROKE HIS THUMB IN FIGHT

He Also Sprained His Right Wrist on Dempsey's Jaw in Second Round

NOT OFFERED AS EXCUSE

BLOW TO THE JAW ENDS THE CONTEST

Story of the Fight by Rounds Shows the Superiority of Dempsey.

ONLY ONCE IN DISTRESS

DEMPSEY PROVES PROWESS

Forces Carpentier Down With Incessant Rain of Terrific Blows.

TWICE FLOORS OPPONENT

But Frenchman Is Courageous After First Knockdown and Fights Until Knocked Out.

NO "ACCIDENTAL CHAMPION"

Great Throng That Gave Louder Cheer for Georges at Start Acclaims Jack at the End.

© 2026 The New York Times Company | Terms of Service | Privacy | Help

FIGURE 14-1: The heavyweight title bout between Jack Dempsey and Georges Carpentier was front-page news . . .

Courtesy of The New York Times Company

Up until the late 1990s, boxing fans still had a variety of print publications from which to receive their fight news. In the 1920s, Ernest Hemingway, Ed Sullivan, Paul Gallico, Grantland Rice, and many others covered boxing on a regular basis. In the 1950s, a magazine as staid as *The New Yorker* employed A. J. Liebling, an esteemed war correspondent, to write scholarly and humorous essays about the likes of Joe Louis, Rocky Marciano, and Sugar Ray Robinson. The tradition continued through the '60s, '70s, and '80s with newspaper and magazine journalists such as Red Smith, Dick Young, Jimmy Cannon, Barney Nagler, Pat Putnam, and Michael Katz specializing in the coverage of professional boxing. And beginning with the establishment of *The Ring* magazine in 1926, a golden age of boxing magazines was launched.

But once network television began cutting back on boxing coverage in the early '90s, so, too, did newspaper and magazine coverage of the fight game begin to dwindle. Publications such as *Boxing Digest, Boxing Illustrated,* and *KO* (see Figure 14-2) gradually died off, and even *The Ring*, established in 1922 to coincide with the rise of Jack Dempsey, went through troubled times and several ownership changes.

FIGURE 14-2: Boxing magazines thrived from the 1920s to the 1990s.

The Ring still survives, and even thrives, under the new ownership of Turki Alalshikh, who has also promoted several fight cards under *The Ring's* banner. It's a handsome publication with great photos and graphics and well worth reading for boxing fans. Other notable print publications include the British-based *Boxing News* (see Figure 14-3), established in 1909; *Boxing Scene,* a US-based publication that employs some of the few truly experienced boxing writers left; and *Uppercut,* a Los Angeles–based publication that specializes in coverage of West Coast Latino boxers. All are available in both print and online editions and provide easy access to fight results, upcoming schedules, and current rankings. In addition to the rankings of the major boxing organizations, *The Ring* publishes its own rankings and recognizes its own champions. *The Ring's* extensive monthly ratings analysis is must-reading for any serious boxing fan.

`Boxrec.com` is the place to go to find out the career record of just about every man or woman who has ever had a boxing match, professional or amateur. The staff is scrupulous in maintaining as accurate an accounting of boxing records as can be found in a sport so fragmented and, frankly, disorganized. The website also includes a schedule of upcoming bouts; information on trainers, managers, and promoters; and a discussion forum for boxing fans.

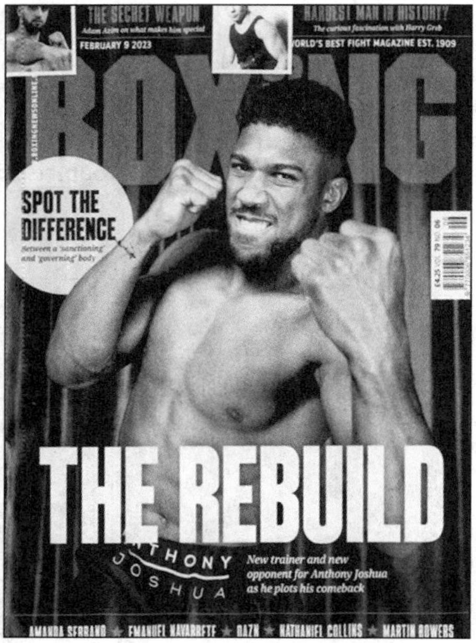

FIGURE 14-3: The British-based *Boxing News* continues to publish both print and online editions.

Courtesy of Boxing News

Watching the Fights

These days, the options for watching fights live are rather limited. While boxing was a staple on weekend television in the 1970s and '80s, boxing has not been regularly featured on network television since 2018, when a partnership between NBC and Premier Boxing Champions expired. In June 2025, ESPN, a cable TV broadcaster, announced that it, too, was dropping boxing after an association of more than two decades.

That left boxing fans with two options — pay for a streaming service such as DAZN, or catch (an often bootlegged) replay of a fight on the Internet the next day. In 2025, the average price for a pay-per-view boxing match ranged from $50 to $100, and a monthly subscription to DAZN, a sports streaming service that often presents major boxing matches, cost $45 per month.

Netflix and Amazon Prime have also entered the boxing streaming service, with Netflix offering the Mike Tyson–Jake Paul fight to its subscribers as a loss leader. Other streaming services, such as `PPV.com` and `PPVNetwork.com`, offer one-time pay-per-view fights without requiring a long-term subscription.

Now, the tough part . . .

Understanding What You're Watching

Most people believe that judging a boxing match is a subjective process, and in many cases it is, often influenced by the observer's personal preferences in terms of fighting style. However, some definite criteria exist by which fights are supposed to be judged, and an understanding of them will help you become a more knowledgeable fan and a more accurate judge. In addition to the innovation of punch-counting programs, which can be a useful aid but by no means should be the sole criteria for judging a fight, boxing judges are trained to use four distinct yardsticks when determining the winner of a bout.

Developing Your Street Cred: How to Watch and Score a Fight

The great former trainer-turned-TV fight analyst Gil Clancy once told me, "You don't need judges to know who won a fight. All you need is to ask a little kid to watch it."

Clancy's point was that it's usually obvious which boxer won the fight and that judges — and fans — sometimes tend to overthink it, rely on preconceived notions of the two fighters, or give too much weight to one aspect of the bout and not enough to another. Children, he maintained, had the ability to just look at two boxers going at it without prejudice and decide who won.

He was right, of course, but unfortunately there's a bit more to it than that when watching a professional boxing match. Professional boxing judges are expected to judge a bout using four criteria:

- Effective aggression
- Defense
- Clean punching
- Ring generalship

Clean punching is pretty much self-explanatory: legal blows that strike a boxer with the knuckle portion of the glove without grazing or glancing off the target or being partially blocked by the gloves or arms.

So, too, is *defense*, the ability to avoid being hit with clean punches, either by movement of the head or body or by blocking with the gloves and arms.

The other two criteria, however, can be open to interpretation, and misinterpretation, even by professional judges.

Let's take a closer look at them:

Recognizing effective aggression

The simplest way to judge a fight is just to note which boxer is landing more punches. This is the basis for the innovative and widely used statistical device known as PunchStat, developed in the 1980s by Bob Canobbio and Logan Hobson under the name of CompuBox Inc.

This is a very useful tool, especially in amateur boxing, which is scored on a quantitative basis: The boxer who lands more clean punches wins. However, the sheer number of punches landed alone does not determine the winner of a professional boxing match. For one thing, Fighter A might out-land Fighter B significantly for the first nine rounds of a fight — only to get knocked out by a single punch in Round 10. Check out the 1994 heavyweight title fight between Michael Moorer and George Foreman to see what I mean.

For another, a larger volume of light punches is often overcome by a smaller number of more powerful punches. The first fight between Muhammad Ali and Joe Frazier is a prime example of that. Ali landed more punches but the vast majority of effective shots — most notably the left hook that floored Ali in the 15th round — came from Frazier, who deservedly won the decision.

That is where the term *effective aggression* comes in. It means the fighter who is forcing the action and whose blows are actually hurting the other fighter is winning the fight, even if they're being outpunched in raw numbers. It's not always easy to gauge the effectiveness of punches while watching a bout on television or to really sense which fighter is forcing the fight, but these are the factors that should determine who is actually winning.

Gauging ring generalship

Ring generalship is a term that refers to a boxer's ability to control the action in the ring, including where the bout is fought — in the middle of the ring, along the ropes or in the corner, at long range or in close — and the tempo it's being fought at.

The legendary boxer Sam Langford, who battled in the early 1900s, described ring generalship this way: "Whatever the other man wants to do, don't let him do it."

That means if a boxer's opponent wants to box, you must force him to brawl. If he wants to brawl, draw him into a boxing match. The boxer who is determining how and where the fight is being fought is demonstrating ring generalship, and that should be factored into your scoring.

Don't sleep on body punches

As discussed in Chapter 9, boxing judges often ignore body punching, either because they're sometimes more difficult to see clearly, or they rarely have an immediate and visible effect the way a solid shot to the jaw does. Also, many judges, never having stepped into a ring, may be ignorant of the way a good body shot affects the boxer being hit.

But body punches are often more painful and energy-sapping than head shots, and a thudding punch to the midsection should be given the same weight as a flashy left hook to the chin. Impress your friends with your understanding of pro boxing by respecting the fighter who effectively works the body, a rapidly vanishing art these days.

Understanding the 10-point must system

Since 2001, all boxing matches have been scored under what is known as the 10-point must system. This means that the winner of a round receives 10 points and the loser receives nine or less, depending on how one-sided the round was. Generally speaking, a standard round in which one boxer is superior to the other will be scored 10–9. If there is a knockdown in the round, it's usually scored 10–8, but there are exceptions: Let's say Fighter A is clearly winning a round but suffers a flash knockdown. Many judges will score that a 10–9 round for the boxer scoring the knockdown. On the other hand, rounds in which a boxer is knocked down multiple times may be scored 10–7 or even, in rare cases, 10–6.

Another exception is if the boxer winning the round is penalized a point by the referee for repeated low blows or some other rules infraction. In that case, despite winning the round, the boxer being penalized has to settle for a 9–9 round. And in the case of a very close round, judges will award a 10–10 round.

But in most cases, rounds will be scored 10–9, and at the end of a 12-round fight, you see scores such as 116–112 or 120–108. All that means is that in the former case, the winning boxer won four more rounds than the loser, hence the four-point difference. In the latter case, the winning fighter was judged to have won every round of the fight.

Punch-counting programs

In the mid-1980s, a punch-counting program known as CompuBox was established by Bob Canobbio and Logan Hobson. It was a system by which two people sat at ringside before a computer keyboard, each assigned to watch one of the fighters. In its infancy, the program was designed to track just two punches — jabs thrown and landed, and power punches (anything other than a jab) thrown and landed. At the end of the bout, each fighter would have a cumulative score. For instance, Fighter A outjabbed Fighter B 120-99, but Fighter B landed more power punches, 75-62.

This was a useful tool in that it added an element of quantitative analysis to a sport notoriously short on statistics other than a fighter's won-loss record, and in many ways, it changed the way boxing was presented and reported on. It was adopted by just about every broadcast outlet and remains an integral part of every boxing broadcast to this day.

But the sheer number of punches thrown and landed does not necessarily determine the winner of a bout. Example: Muhammad Ali clearly landed more punches than Joe Frazier in their epic 1971 heavyweight title showdown, but anyone who watched the fight knew that Frazier had won. That is because relying solely on the volume of punches does not account for their effectiveness or lack thereof, and as we saw earlier, effective punching is a key criteria for judging a bout.

So when watching a fight, it is OK to be cognizant of who is throwing and landing more punches, but always remember that it is the *effective* punches that truly count.

After all, a boxer can outland his opponent 10 punches to 1 for 11 rounds and be knocked out by a single punch in round 12. To see what I mean, check out the 1994 George Foreman–Michael Moorer heavyweight title fight, won by Foreman on a one-punch KO in round 10 after having lost every previous round.

A handy way to score a fight

During my years as a boxing writer, I devised a system to keep track of what was going on in the ring by means of a simple self-made scorecard similar to the type used to score a baseball game.

In Figure 14-4, you see that the scorecard consists of two rows, one for each boxer, followed by boxes for each of the scheduled rounds of the fight. Alongside each boxer's name I would write their official weight as announced at the pre-fight weigh-in, and below the name the boxer's record with the number of KOs in parentheses.

The boxes for each round of the fight were divided by a diagonal line, which allowed me to document, in the top half, who (in my opinion) won any particular round, and the cumulative total of the bout in the bottom half.

I would sketch this grid at the top of a sheet of legal-size paper, leaving space below the grid to add notes and observations about each round.

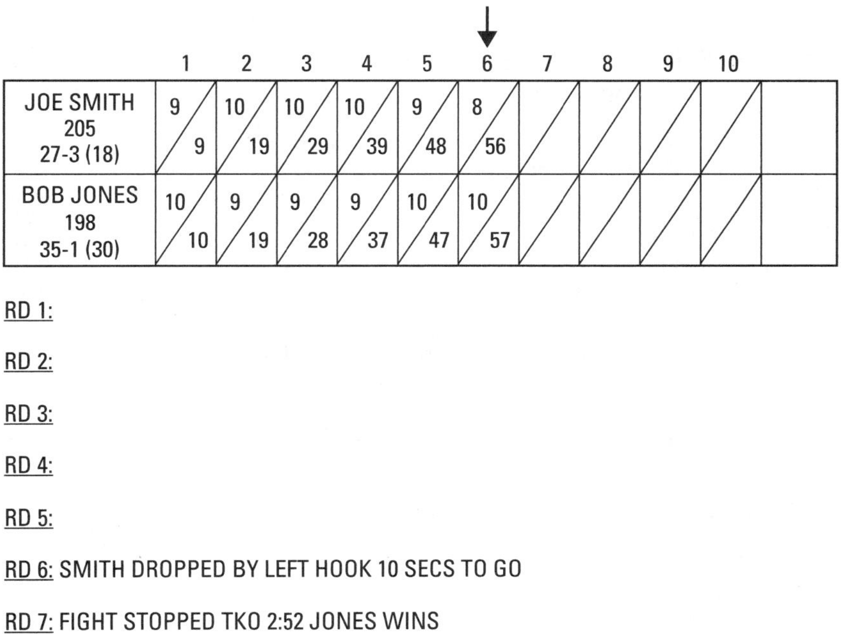

FIGURE 14-4: This simple grid-type scorecard makes it easy to keep track of who you think is winning a fight.

Knowing the rules

The basic rules of professional boxing, as established in 2001 by the Association of Boxing Commissions, are as follows:

- Rounds are three minutes long, with one-minute rest periods.
- The referee is the sole arbiter of the rules and the only one who can stop a fight.
- All bouts will be scored by three ringside judges using the 10-point must system.
- All boxers being knocked down will be given a mandatory eight-count before continuing.

- All boxers scoring a knockdown will retreat to the furthest neutral corner.
- There is no standing eight-count or three-knockdown rule.
- All boxers must wear a mouthpiece and if the mouthpiece is dislodged, the referee will stop the action and replace it. Intentionally spitting out a mouthpiece to get a rest is a foul and punishable by points deduction.
- A knocked-down boxer cannot be saved by the bell in any round. The count will continue after the bell.
- A boxer who cannot continue following an injury from a legal blow will be judged a loser by technical knockout (TKO).
- A boxer who is injured by a foul and cannot continue will be awarded a victory by disqualification.
- If an intentional foul causes an injury and the bout is allowed to continue, the referee shall deduct two points from the boxer who caused the foul.
- If an intentional foul causes an injury and the bout is allowed to continue, and the injury results in the bout being stopped in any round after the fourth round, if the injured boxer is ahead on the score cards, they will be ruled the winner by a technical decision.
- If the injured boxer is behind or even on the score cards, the result of the bout will be a technical draw.
- If an accidental foul causes an injury severe enough for the referee to stop the bout, the bout will result in a NO DECISION if stopped before four completed rounds. Four rounds are complete when the bell rings, signifying the end of the fourth round.
- If an accidental foul causes an injury severe enough for the referee to stop the bout after four rounds have occurred, the bout will result in a TECHNICAL DECISION awarded to the boxer who is ahead on the score cards at the time the bout is stopped.
- A fighter who is hit with an accidental low blow must continue after a reasonable amount of time but no more than five minutes, or they will lose the fight.
- Hitting below the belt, hitting on the break, hitting after the bell, rabbit punching, backhand punching, and excessive clinching or holding can result in points deductions and disqualification if done repeatedly after warnings from the referee.

Talking the talk

In boxing as in every sport, there is a certain lingo that if you know, you know, and if you don't, well, everyone else will know.

For instance, when discussing the weight of a fighter, never use the words "**One Hundred**" and avoid using the weight class. That means when discussing a welterweight, say **"He's a 47."** When discussing a lightweight, **"He's a 35."** And so on. This establishes your bona fides as someone who knows the game.

Other things to know:

- When two fighters of different weight classes agree to meet somewhere in the middle, for instance a light-heavyweight (**"a 75"**) and a middleweight (**"a 60"**) agreeing to fight at **"68,"** they are said to be fighting at **catch weights.**
- **Walking down:** Forcing an opponent backwards by pressure with the intention of trapping them on the ropes or in a corner.
- **Tying up:** Preventing an opponent from punching by clinching or wrapping your arms around them. Excessive clinching is a foul.
- **Covering up:** A fighter is raising their arms and gloves in front of their face with the intention not of delivering punches, but blocking them. This is also known as going into a **clamshell,** or in hockey**, turtling up.**
- **Hurt** doesn't mean what you think it does. Although taking punches is certainly painful, when boxers talk about being hurt, they are referring to being mentally discombobulated, shook up, or, in extreme cases, close to being knocked out.
- A fighter who lands flurries of quick but not especially hard punches is said to be **doing a paint job** on his opponent.
- **Shoeshining:** Delivering a fast series of punches to the body, so-called because the motion resembles that of buffing your shoes with a cloth.
- **Runner:** A fighter who prefers not to stand his ground and fight. These fighters are often said to be **on the bicycle.**
- **Bleeder:** A fighter who cuts easily.
- **Plodder:** A fighter who is slow on their feet.
- **Bricklayer:** A fighter with a powerful punch. These fighters are sometimes said to be **heavy-handed.**
- **Slapper**: A boxer who tends to land his punches with the palm of his glove rather than his knuckles.

- **Arm puncher:** A boxer who throws his punches without the weight of his body behind them.
- A boxer who has enough power to overcome a points deficit with a single punch late in a bout is said to possess **the equalizer.**
- **Chinny:** A fighter who does not take a punch well.
- **Tomato can, palooka,** and **opponent:** Derogatory terms used to describe fighters who are not very good and generally brought in to lose to a local or better-known fighter.
- **Journeyman:** A solid step up from a Tomato Can, Palooka, or Opponent. It usually means a veteran boxer who can be counted on to give a good effort in defeat.
- **Washed, shot,** and **a punched ticket:** Terms used to describe a fighter whose skills have eroded and is ready for retirement.
- **Dive:** When a fighter deliberately loses a bout. Also known as **going into the water.**
- The major boxing sanctioning organizations — the WBC, WBA, and IBF — are known collectively and often disparagingly as **the alphabets.**
- **Tuna fish belt:** A belt held by a champion whose claim to his title is suspect, hence the insinuation that the adornments on his title belt are made up of empty tuna fish cans.

A mastery of these terms buys you instant street cred among any group of boxing aficionados.

IN THIS CHAPTER

» What a promoter does

» What a manager does

» How does a boxer get paid?

» Who does a boxer have to pay?

» What exactly is a boxing ring anyway?

Chapter 15

Looking at How It All Works

When you watch a major boxing match, several questions might occur to you aside from who is going to win the fight. To wit, who is this person who calls himself the promoter, and what does he do?

OK, so you've heard the main event boxers are getting millions of dollars each for their night's work. Where exactly does that money come from? And how does it finally get to the boxers?

Who are those people in the boxer's corner, and what are they doing there?

And what exactly is this roped square in which it all takes place?

The Ring: The Boxer's Office

You probably already know that boxing matches take place in what is called a ring. The name implies a circle but the ring is in fact a square and bordered by four ropes that are intended to keep the boxers safely within that square. Like professional baseball fields, boxing rings can vary in size, from 16 to 24 feet square, depending upon the rules of the controlling jurisdiction and often, the size of the venue in which the fight is being held. The most common size is 20 feet square within the ropes. All rings are bordered with an apron that extends two feet beyond the ropes on all sides to prevent a boxer who slips through the ropes from falling to the floor. (See Figure 15-1.)

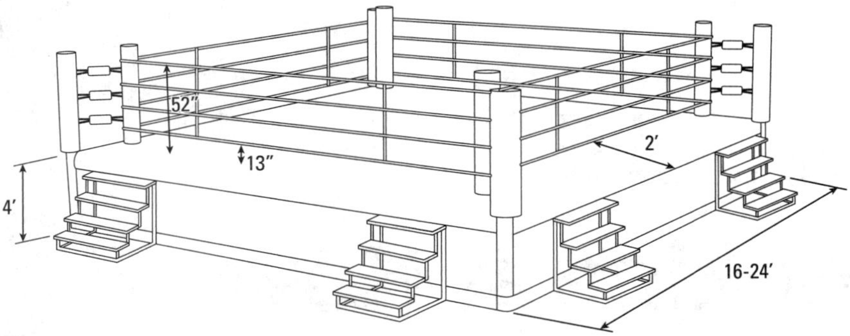

FIGURE 15-1: A typical boxing ring.

The floor of a boxing ring is a firmly padded foam rubber surface covered by a tightly stretched canvas. The boxing ring is not bouncy like the rings used for professional wrestling; the bounce you see comes solely from the legs of the boxer.

The ring ropes are covered with a nonabrasive material and spaced at 13-inch intervals, with the top rope sitting 52 inches above the ring surface. The ropes are supported by posts in each corner and tightened by turnbuckles, which are covered with vertical foam pads, called corner pads, to keep a boxer driven into a corner from being injured. The ring surface is four feet above the ground.

One corner is assigned to each boxer and their seconds, diagonally across from each other. The two unassigned corners are called *neutral corners*. These are the areas to which a fighter scoring a knockdown is directed to go by the referee before he begins his count over a downed boxer.

Behind the Scenes

In boxing, it takes two to tangle, but it takes a lot more than just the boxers to get a major fight off the ground. There's the promoter, who puts the whole thing together; the athletic commission, which regulates the bout; the site that hosts the bout; the publicists, who get the word out to the media; the writers and broadcasters, who get it to the public; and, of course, all the members of each boxer's training camp (the manager, trainer, conditioning coach, nutritionist, sparring partners, and so on).

Let's take a closer look at what each of them actually does to make Fight Night a reality.

What does a promoter do?

Every boxing event has a *promoter*, who is similar to a movie producer or anyone whose responsibility it is to stage a big event. Simply put, the promoter's job is to come up with a marketable boxing match, find a place to hold it, rustle up the money to stage it, determine how much it will cost to produce and how much he would like to put in his own pocket, and negotiate the payments to the main event fighters.

Tex Rickard was boxing's first major promoter, staging multiple fights featuring heavyweight champion Jack Dempsey in the 1920s that drew more than 100,000 spectators and generated more than $1 million at the gate. Rickard's successors were Mike Jacobs, who promoted bouts at New York City's Madison Square Garden in the 1940s and '50s; Don King and Bob Arum, who dominated boxing in the '70s, '80s, and '90s and moved it from the urban arena into more lucrative casino venues; and currently, Eddie Hearn, Al Haymon, and Turki Alalshikh, who have ventured into the oil-rich Mideast.

Where does the promoter get the money?

In the pre-broadcast era, the revenue streams for the earliest boxing promoters were limited to ticket sales and concessions at the live arena, which is why fights in the '20s and '30s were held in huge outdoor venues, and often in the daytime because of the absence of artificial light in many arenas.

The first major boxing match to be broadcast over the radio was the 1921 heavyweight title fight between Dempsey and Georges Carpentier, which still drew 91,000 fans to Boyle's Thirty Acres in Jersey City. Later, promoters found another revenue stream, the delayed showing of the fight film in a movie theater.

By 1939, television was getting into the act. The first major fight televised in the United States was a heavyweight bout between former champion Max Baer and Lou Nova.

The advent of television provided a windfall for boxing promoters, although it had an adverse effect on the live gate, since many fans preferred to remain home and watch the fight for free rather than pay for a ticket.

The first televised heavyweight title fight was the 1946 rematch between Joe Louis and Billy Conn, won by Louis on a sixth-round knockout. The first major bout to be presented on closed-circuit television and shown in movie theaters was the 1948 heavyweight title bout between Joe Louis and Jersey Joe Walcott. This was the forerunner of what we know today as pay-per-view television, which nowadays is the main revenue stream for modern boxing promoters.

But through the early 1980s, there was plenty of boxing on free television, beginning with weekly fights sponsored by companies such as Gillette razor blades and Pabst Blue Ribbon beer. In the 1970s and '80s, fights featuring such luminaries as Muhammad Ali, Larry Holmes, Marvin Hagler, and Sugar Ray Leonard were available on weekend afternoon television shows such as ABC's Wide World of Sports and CBS Sports Spectacular. Because of its nature, boxing matches provided built-in commercial breaks between rounds. Ad revenue from those commercials became part of the revenue stream available to a boxing promoter to produce the event.

In the late 1980s, subscription cable networks such as ESPN, HBO, and Showtime began presenting boxing matches, adding an additional revenue stream to boxing promoters.

In 1971, the first fight between Muhammad Ali and Joe Frazier, billed as "The Fight of the Century," drew a worldwide audience of 300 million people, who paid to watch the fight live in a movie theater via closed-circuit television. Although some earlier championship fights had been presented on closed-circuit television, Ali–Frazier I ushered in a new era of televised boxing.

By the late 1980s, pay-per-view boxing had moved from the theater to the living room, with championship fights available on your home TV screen for a price. The first pay-per-view fights cost approximately $40. By 2025 the prices ranged from $60 to over $100, depending on the event. Other sources of revenue include the site fee, the amount a venue will pay to host a fight, foreign rights fees, streaming services, sponsorships, and the sale of fight-related merchandise. These additional revenue streams have made it possible for boxers such as Mike Tyson to be paid a then-unprecedented $30 million for a single fight (his 1997 TKO loss to Evander Holyfield) and for Mexico's Canelo Alvarez, a champion in four weight classes, to sign an 11-fight deal paying him $365 million.

These greatly increased revenue streams have had a profound effect on the earning power of today's most popular boxers. In 2018, *Forbes* magazine named Floyd Mayweather Jr. the world's highest-paid athlete, with earnings estimated at $285 million. In recent years, heavyweight Tyson Fury has earned upward of $200 million, Oleksandr Usyk earned more than $132 million, and Jake Paul, a YouTube celebrity, earned approximately $100 million for fighting former heavyweight champion Anthony Joshua, a fight he lost by knockout.

Who decides who is fighting whom?

High-profile main title fights pretty much make themselves, either by popular demand (Muhammad Ali and Joe Frazier, for example) or by decree of one of the sanctioning organizations, which designates a boxer as its number one contender and gives its champion a deadline by which they must fight. But promoters also employ *matchmakers,* whose job it is to fill out the rest of the boxing card with suitable fights. Teddy Brenner, a legendary matchmaker who worked for Madison Square Garden and later for Bob Arum, once described his job as "Let's you and him fight." A good matchmaker designs a boxing event so that the undercard fights build the excitement and anticipation for the main bout, generally the last or second-to-last bout on the card.

Anyone else?

A boxing promoter also needs *publicists*, whose job is to get the word out to media outlets that the fight is happening, and *site coordinators,* who work with the chosen venue to make sure all the logistics such as the ring, the lighting, the safety requirements, the fighters' accommodations, and the media arrangements are in place by fight week.

Let's follow the money

The modern-day promoter dreams up a match between Fighter A and Fighter B. He then makes an educated guess about probable ticket sales and all the other revenue streams the match is likely to attract. Based on that estimate, the promoter begins to raise the required money. He brings it to a *site* such as a casino hotel or an arena and negotiates a site fee or a percentage of ticket sales. He presents it to a television outlet or a streaming service. He offers the rights to televise the fight to promoters in Europe, Asia, South America, and Australia. He sells the merchandising rights for fight T-shirts and other collectibles, and attempts to procure sponsorships from beer and liquor companies, boxing equipment manufacturers, and basically anyone else who would like to cash in. He sells advertising on the ring canvas, the corner pads, and the cards carried overhead between rounds, usually by scantily clad young women, to remind the fans what round is coming up.

All of this goes into the pot, at which point the promoter calculates the amount of money he hopes to raise, and then makes an offer to the two fighters — or more likely, to their managers or business advisors. After all the expenses are paid, the promoter takes his profit. Or if the fight fails at the box office, he takes a loss.

The only ones guaranteed a payday are the fighters. But the amount the promoter offers to the fighter is a gross amount, not take-home pay. Out of it, the fighter must pay his manager (traditionally 33 percent), his trainer (10 percent), and any other conditioning or nutritional coaches he chooses to employ, as well as other members of his "entourage." In big fights, the boxers may be given an allowance for training expenses, but often that comes out of the fighter's share, too. And then, of course, Uncle Sam has his hand out. You can see how what appears to be a huge payday can quickly be whittled down to much less. After paying expenses and taxes, a fighter generally walks away with about 40 percent of the contracted purse. And in return for being offered the match, a promoter will sometimes require the boxer to sign an option on future fights.

High-earning fighters such as Sugar Ray Leonard, Oscar de la Hoya, Manny Pacquiao, and Floyd Mayweather Jr. were powerful enough to circumvent the system, employing lawyers or business managers rather than traditional fight managers, to whom they would pay a negotiated fee rather than a set percentage of their earnings. They would do the same with their trainers. And since the promoters needed them more than vice versa, they were able to remain free agents, fighting for whom they wanted to against whom they cared to fight. Alas, this is not the case for the average boxer.

THE MUHAMMAD ALI BOXING REFORM ACT

The exploitation of professional boxers by promoters, managers, and state athletic commissions has gone on throughout the history of the sport. In May 2000, following several years of hearings and testimony from numerous boxing luminaries spearheaded by the late senator (and former boxer) John McCain, the Muhammad Ali Boxing Reform Act became federal law.

Its purpose was both to protect boxers from financial exploitation and to ensure their safety. Quoting directly from the Congressional Record of the 106th Congress, the stated aims of the Muhammad Ali act were:

- To protect the rights and welfare of professional boxers on an interstate basis by preventing certain exploitive, oppressive, and unethical business practices
- To assist state boxing commissions in their efforts to provide more effective public oversight of the sport
- To promote honorable competition in professional boxing and enhance the overall integrity of the industry

Among those called upon to testify were former heavyweight champion Mike Tyson, a strong proponent of the bill, who testified he had been bilked out of some $65 million in earnings; boxing promoters Bob Arum, who supported the act, and Don King, who opposed it; referee Mills Lane; and Muhammad Ali himself. I was among a handful of boxing journalists called to give testimony, during which I told the senators that the only people who could truly educate them on how to effectively reform boxing were the people who were benefiting from the current system — namely, the promoters, managers, and state commissions.

Among the provisions of the law was the prohibition of requiring boxers to sign long-term contracts with a promoter in exchange for getting a title shot, the forcing of boxers to sign managerial contracts with a manager associated with or related to a promoter (many of the boxers promoted by Don King were managed by his son, Carl), and full financial disclosure of all sources of revenue for a bout. Previously, boxers were not privy to such information and might not know that a promoter had raised $1 million for their bout while paying only $50,000 in purses.

The Ali Act also provided for reciprocity among state commissions, meaning that a fighter under disciplinary or medical suspension in one state could not be licensed to fight in another state until the original suspension was lifted.

If properly enforced, such provisions would have provided much-needed protection to professional boxers. However, the Ali Act lacked teeth — the American Association of Boxing Commissions, the nominal overseer of the state athletic commissions, was given no real enforcement power other than to "suggest" that all commissions follow these guidelines. As a result, "numerous violations of the Ali Act went unpunished," according to Thomas Hauser of ESPN.

In 2025, a bill was introduced in Congress to amend the Ali Act, driven mainly by promoters of mixed martial arts events. The proposed amendment would establish UBOs — Unified Boxing Organizations — which would take the place of the established sanctioning bodies (WBA, WBC, IBF, and IBO). The proposed amendment called for minimum per-round payments, mandatory medical examinations, and expanded health insurance, but also sought to eliminate financial disclosure of event revenue to boxers. The bill has been supported by Tyson and opposed by USA Boxing, the national governing body for amateur boxing in the United States, and former boxing champion and current promoter Oscar de la Hoya.

The act was passed by the House of Representatives in March of 2026 and at the time of this writing, hearings on it were being held in the Senate.

HOW BOXING REVENUE HAS CHANGED THROUGH THE YEARS

JACK DEMPSEY – GEORGES CARPENTIER

Venue: Boyle's Thirty Acres, Jersey City, New Jersey

Date: July 2, 1921

Attendance: 80,000

Fighter's purses: Dempsey $300,000 plus 25 percent of motion picture rights; Carpentier: $200,000 plus 25 percent of motion picture rights

Ticket sales: $1,789,238 (tickets priced from $5.50 to $50)

MUHAMMAD ALI – JOE FRAZIER I

Venue: Madison Square Garden, New York City

Date: March 8, 1971

Attendance: 20,455

Fighter's purses: $2.5 million each

Site fee: None

Ticket sales: $1.5 million (tickets priced from $20 to $150)

Closed-circuit TV revenue: $45 million (seats priced from $5 to $15)

Foreign broadcast rights: $20 million

Viewership: 300 million worldwide (est.)

The purses were guaranteed by Jack Kent Cooke ($4.5 million) and Madison Square Garden ($500,000). With the business of boxing matches shown live in movie theaters via closed-circuit TV still in its infancy, Ali and Frazier opted to take guaranteed purses rather than a percentage of the gross revenue, which would have paid them millions more.

MARVELOUS MARVIN HAGLER – SUGAR RAY LEONARD

Venue: Caesars Palace, Las Vegas, Nevada

Date: April 6, 1987

Attendance: 15,000

Fighter's purses: Hagler $12 million guaranteed, plus a percentage of other revenues (estimated $20 million gross); Leonard $11 million guaranteed, plus 50 percent of the closed-circuit television rights in Maryland and the District of Columbia (estimated $12 million gross)

Site fee: $6.8 million

Ticket sales: $7.8 million (tickets priced from $40 to $700). Closed-circuit and pay-per-view telecasts cost $35 to $40.

Other revenue (closed-circuit and PPV TV, foreign broadcast rights, sponsorships, merchandising, delayed broadcast rights): Approximately $60 million

Viewership: Exact number unknown; available to approximately three million US homes via pay-per-view TV and approximately 1,500 closed-circuit TV locations in the US and Canada

FLOYD MAYWEATHER JR. – MANNY PACQUIAO

Venue: MGM Grand Garden Arena, Las Vegas, Nevada

Date: May 2, 2015

Attendance: 16,800 (Only 500 tickets sold to the general public at prices ranging from $1,500 to $7,500. The rest were allocated to hotel casinos for distribution to their guests.)

Fighter's purses: Mayweather $180 million; Pacquiao $120 million

Site fee: None

Ticket sales: $72.2 million

Pay-per-view TV sales: 4.4 million, generating $400 million in revenue

(continued)

(continued)

Additional revenue streams: Foreign TV rights, sponsorship, merchandising, and the like added another $100 million.

Note: Mayweather and Pacquiao split all gross revenue above $180 million on a 60/40 basis, with Mayweather getting the larger share.

TERENCE CRAWFORD – SAUL (CANELO) ALVAREZ

Venue: Allegiant Stadium, Las Vegas, Nevada

Date: September 13, 2025

Attendance: 70,482

Fighter's purses: Crawford $10 million guaranteed (reportedly $50 million with ancillary rights); Alvarez $100–150 million as part of a $400 million promotional contract with Saudi Arabian–based promoter Riyadh Season

Site fee: None

Ticket sales: Approximately $47 million (tickets priced from $381 to $1,669)

Pay-per-view TV: None; streamed live on Netflix free to its subscribers

Viewership: Approximately 41 million

Note: Adjusted for inflation, $1 in 1971 dollars is roughly equivalent to $8.20 in 2026; $1 in 1987 is roughly equivalent to $2.93 in 2026.

So Who Really Decides Who the Champions Are?

Ever since Muhammad Ali refused induction into the US Army on religious grounds in 1967, boxing has been a mess. Within hours of Ali's refusal to take the ceremonial step forward on April 28, 1967, the New York State Athletic Commission suspended his license to box and the World Boxing Association stripped Ali of his heavyweight title. Soon, other US boxing commissions followed suit and Ali was unable to get a license to box for more than three years.

This spawned the beginning of the fragmentation of boxing titles that has mushroomed into the current situation: At the time of this writing, there were four major boxing sanctioning organizations, each recognizing their own champions in 17 weight classes. As a result, 47 different men were calling themselves "world champions" with only one, Japanese junior featherweight (122 pounds) Naoya Inoue, recognized by all four organizations. Over the past two decades, only 11 men and 13 women have been recognized as world champions by all four organizations, and generally for only short periods of time. In addition, one organization, the WBA, now recognizes three different champions in each weight class. To save your sanity, don't ask how or why!

The inability to identify one boxer as the true champion in any weight class has caused confusion and frustration among boxing fans, and no doubt contributed greatly to boxing's decline in popularity as a spectator sport. Since there is no central organization governing all of boxing such as the National Football League and Major League Baseball, the sanctioning organizations operate autonomously and have been accused of corruption and favoritism in the ranking of their boxers and the recognition of their champions. All four organizations collect "sanctioning fees," which can run into the hundreds of thousands of dollars, from promoters in exchange for its recognition of a bout as a title contest.

That is why all boxing rankings should be viewed skeptically, and all discerning boxing fans should form their own judgments on the merits of a contender and the legitimacy of a champion based upon educated observation. Better to call them "title holders" than champions.

That being said, here are the four major boxing sanctioning organizations as recognized by the International Boxing Hall of Fame in Canastota, New York.

The World Boxing Association (WBA)

The World Boxing Association was formed in the United States in 1921 as the National Boxing Association but relocated to Panama City in the 1970s. The WBA was the first to strip Ali of his title and created a tournament to crown his successor. The tournament was won by Jimmy Ellis, but New York State refused to recognize Ellis, sanctioning a "title fight" between Buster Mathis and Joe Frazier, who withdrew from the WBA tournament. Frazier won, beginning the era of split titles that has persisted to this day. And in the 1980s, several boxing promoters alleged having to bribe WBA president Gilberto Mendoza in exchange for having their fighters ranked.

The World Boxing Council (WBC)

In 1963, 11 countries, including the United States, met in Mexico City to establish the World Boxing Council. The WBC was instrumental in reducing the length of championship bouts from 15 to 12 rounds following the death of Duk-Koo Kim in a 1983 bout with Ray Mancini, and was among the first to recognize women boxers Christy Martin and Lucia Rijker as world champions. But in the late 1980s it was alleged that the WBC and its president, Jose Sulaiman, provided preferential treatment to boxers promoted by Don King. Today, Sulaiman's son, Mauricio, serves as the organization's president and their championship belt remains highly coveted.

The International Boxing Federation (IBF)

Established in 1983 as a US-based alternative to the WBA and WBC, the International Boxing Federation, formerly the United States Boxing Association, gained legitimacy in 1984 when Larry Holmes relinquished his WBC heavyweight title and accepted the IBF's belt. In 1999, the IBF was racked by scandal when promoter Bob Arum testified he had paid its president, Bob Lee, a $100,000 bribe to sanction a title fight between champion George Foreman and challenger Axel Schulz, Darryl Peoples, the current president of the IBF, has restored the organization to a level of respectability.

The World Boxing Organization (WBO)

The "new kid on the block," the WBO was formed in 1988 by a splinter group of Puerto Rican and Dominican businessmen formerly associated with the WBA. The WBO gained respectability by electing Jose Torres, an ex–light heavyweight champion and former chair of the New York State Athletic Commission, as its president. But rather than reduce the confusion among fight fans, the WBO only added to it by establishing "super champions" in addition to its roster of champions in 17 weight classes.

The Ring Magazine Ratings

The Ring is the oldest continuously published boxing magazine, established in 1922. In 1924, *The Ring* began publishing its own independent boxing ratings and recognizing its own world champions, although these, too, were somewhat tainted since the original set of ratings were approved by Tex Rickard, the sport's major promoter of the 1920s. But since the 1980s, the ratings have been determined by a panel of journalists from around the world. Currently *The Ring* rates male boxers in 17 weight classes and female boxers in 16 weight classes. Its ratings are considered by some fans to be the most legitimate because they are ostensibly not influenced by promoters, nor does the publication collect sanctioning fees from promoters or boxers.

IN THIS CHAPTER

» Understanding the difference between professional and amateur boxing

» Learning the history and legacy of USA Boxing

» Recognizing the globalization of boxing

Chapter 16

Keeping Tabs on the Amateurs

There was a time in the not-too-distant past when boxing successfully as an amateur was a sure road to fame and riches in professional boxing. Local Golden Gloves tournaments, the Pan Am Games, and, of course, the Olympic Games were major showcases for young boxers with aspirations of turning professional and catching the eye of an established boxing manager or promoter.

That dynamic has changed somewhat over the past two decades but a competitive amateur boxing background is still considered a solid foundation for anyone pursuing a career in professional boxing or, truly, just about any field in which discipline, determination, and problem-solving skills are requirements.

Understanding the Differences between Amateur and Professional Boxing

In both amateur and professional boxing, rounds are three minutes for men, two minutes for women, with a 60-second rest period in between.

But that's about the only thing identical between the two sports. As originally conceived, amateur boxing was nearly identical to professional boxing and served mainly as a sort of minor leagues for aspiring pros. The boxers competed without headgear and the bouts were fought largely with the same intention as a professional bout: to inflict damage upon an opponent and, if possible, score a knockout.

In recent years, however, amateur boxing has adopted some safety measures not used in professional boxing, and has become more oriented toward the scoring of points than the inflicting of damage. To that end, amateur boxers in some international competitions wear boxing gloves with a white area across the knuckles to make it easier for judges to see clean blows.

Amateur boxing matches generally are scheduled for three three-minute rounds (two minutes for women) and since 2016, are scored on the same 10-point must system (explained in Chapter 14) as in professional boxing. Unlike professional boxing matches, which are scored by three judges, international and Olympic boxing matches are scored by five judges.

For a time, amateur boxers in international competition were required to wear headgear. In 1984, following the death of Korean boxer Duk-Koo Kim from injuries sustained in a bout against lightweight champion Ray Mancini two years earlier, the International Boxing Association (AIBA) mandated headgear for male boxers. That mandate was rescinded for male boxers in 2016 based upon research suggesting the wearing of headgear might actually increase the possibility of concussion. Due to lack of evidence regarding the effectiveness of headguards for female boxers — existing studies were conducted only on male boxers — women amateur boxers are still required to wear headgear.

Going for the Gold: USA Boxing and the Olympics

Boxing is one of the original Olympic sports, dating back to the Games in ancient Greece. But in recent years, allegations of corruption have roiled the sport and, as a result, boxing was in danger of being excluded from the 2028 Los Angeles Olympics for the first time since the 1912 Stockholm Games. (Boxing was banned in Sweden at the time.) But in February 2025, the International Olympic Committee voted to include boxing in the Los Angeles Games.

Between 1904 and 2016, the United States had a long and proud history in Olympic boxing. The first US Olympic boxing champion was George Finnegan, a flyweight (112) at the 1904 Games in St. Louis. Over the next century, boxing became one of the most prestigious events of the Summer Olympics, and the United States has won more boxing gold medals (50) than any other country. Cuba, which has no professional boxing, is second with 41. Cuba has also produced two of the only three Olympic boxers to have won three gold medals, heavyweights Teofilo Stevenson and Felix Savon. The other three-time champion is László Papp, a Hungarian middleweight who later turned professional and was unbeaten in 29 fights when his career came to an abrupt halt. Although signed to fight Joey Giardello for the world championship, Papp was denied an exit visa by the Hungarian government, fearing his defection. Papp never fought professionally again.

Notable US Olympic champions who went on to win professional world titles include Floyd Patterson, who won gold as a middleweight in the 1952 Helsinki Games and later became the first two-time heavyweight champion; Cassius Clay, who won as a light-heavyweight at the 1960 Rome Games and later gained worldwide fame as Muhammad Ali; Joe Frazier, who won gold at the 1960 Tokyo Games and went on to defeat Muhammad Ali in an epic 1971 heavyweight title bout; and George Foreman, who won gold in the 1968 Mexico City Games and dethroned Frazier for the heavyweight title in 1973.

The United States won five gold medals at the 1976 Games in Montreal, three of them won by future world champions Sugar Ray Leonard and Leon and Michael Spinks. History's most successful Olympic boxing team was the US squad of the 1984 Los Angeles Games. Gold medal winners Meldrick Taylor, Pernell Whitaker, and Mark Breland went on to win professional world titles, as did light-heavyweight Evander Holyfield, who was disqualified in a semifinal bout for allegedly hitting on a break.

Mike Tyson, who became the most famous professional heavyweight of the 1980s, did not make the 1984 Olympic team. He was defeated twice in the Olympic Trials by Henry Tillman, whom Tyson later knocked out in one round as a professional.

In recent years, US domination of Olympic boxing has stalled, with Oscar de la Hoya (1992), David Reid (1996), and Andre Ward (2004) the only male gold medalists of the past 35 years.

Women's boxing was added to the 2012 Games in London. The first female gold medalist was flyweight Nicola Adams of Great Britain. At the same Games Claressa Shields of Flint, Michigan, won the first of her two consecutive gold medals and went on to win professional world championships in five weight classes.

Remembering two Olympic boxing scandals

Two of the most infamous Olympic boxing scandals involved US boxers. In 1984, light-heavyweight Evander Holyfield was disqualified when the referee ruled that his left hook, which floored New Zealand's Kevin Barry, was delivered after he had given the order to "stop," which is the amateur equivalent of "break." Ironically, the referee was stopping the action to warn Barry about excessive holding. Barry, who was unable to continue in the bout, was medically barred from further competition and awarded a silver medal. The gold medal was awarded by default to Anton Josipović of Yugoslavia. Holyfield was given a bronze but at the medal ceremony, Josipović pulled Holyfield up to the gold medal podium in tribute.

In 1988, US junior welterweight Roy Jones Jr. was declared the loser in a bout with South Korea's Park Si-Hun, despite having seemingly won all three rounds of the bout. Despite the controversial loss, Jones was awarded the Val Barker Trophy as the best boxer of the Olympics, and following an investigation, all three of the judges who voted against Jones were suspended by AIBA. In 2023, Park Si-Hun gave his gold medal to Jones in acknowledgment of the injustice committed in Seoul.

The 2016 Rio de Janeiro scandal

Allegations of bribery, manipulated scorecards, and rigged results in medal-round bouts tainted the sport at the 2016 Rio de Janeiro Games and resulted in boxing's near exclusion from the 2028 Games. The suspect decisions involved several Russian boxers, including heavyweight Evgeny Tishchenko, awarded a controversial decision over Kazakhstan's Vasily Levit in the gold medal bout, and Vladimir Nikitin, declared the winner over Ireland's Michael Conlan. Although AIBA removed several judges and referees following the unpopular decisions, no results were overturned. An independent investigation turned up evidence of manipulation of a new computer judging system employed for the first time at the Rio Games. AIBA was barred by the International Olympic Committee (IOC) from running the boxing program at the 2020 Tokyo Olympics. The IOC took control of the sport in Tokyo and at the 2024 Paris Games.

Recognizing the globalization of boxing

Amateur boxing, and in particular international and Olympic competition, has played a major role in the globalization of boxing. In 1988, 106 nations sent 432 boxers to the Seoul Olympics, the highest number ever, and despite allegations of scandal and a dwindling of popularity of professional boxing, 68 countries sent 248 boxers to the 2024 Games in Paris. Some of the most notable non-US-born Olympic champions who went on to professional success include Lennox Lewis of Canada, gold medalist in the super-heavyweight class in 1988; Vasily Lomachenko and Oleksandr Usyk, both of Ukraine, who won gold at lightweight and heavyweight respectively in 2012; and Great Britain's Anthony Joshua, super-heavyweight gold medalist at the same Games.

6 The Part of Tens

IN THIS PART . . .

Get acquainted with some fighters all boxing fans should know.

Learn about some important boxing matches, with links to videos available on the web.

Find out about boxing books every fight fan can benefit from by reading.

Get the details about some boxing movies that feature unusual realism both in their storylines and their fight sequences.

Chapter 17

The Dynamic Dozen

As of 2024, there were roughly 8.9 million people participating in boxing at the pro or amateur level in the United States alone, and at the time of this writing (April 2025), some 122 people (73 men and 49 women) hold a claim to some form of a world title due to the proliferation of sanctioning organizations, the splintering of weight classes, and the creation of "interim" and "super" championships.

But relatively few boxers have really changed the way the game is played. Here are a dozen who truly made a difference in boxing history.

Jack Johnson

The first Black heavyweight champion of the world, Jack Johnson, was reviled and eventually exiled from the United States for his flamboyant behavior in and out of the ring, forced to defend his title overseas for the last several years of his five-year title reign. The search to find a Caucasian heavyweight to dethrone Johnson led to the term "Great White Hope." Johnson's fight with former champion James J. Jeffries, the first of the "Hopes," caused race riots around the country when

Johnson scored a brutal 15th-round knockout and resulted in boxing's color line, preventing another Black boxer from winning the title until 1937, when Joe Louis defeated James J. Braddock.

Sugar Ray Robinson

Considered by many, Muhammad Ali included, to be history's greatest all-around boxer, Sugar Ray Robinson (born Walker Smith) won five world titles and 174 fights, 109 by knockout, in a career that spanned 25 years. Over an eight-year stretch (1943–1951), Robinson was unbeaten in 91 consecutive fights.

Muhammad Ali

The man who coined the acronym GOAT — about himself, of course — and backed it up in some of the most famous and dramatic fights in history, Muhammad Ali was the first boxer to hold the heavyweight title three times. His knockouts over Sonny Liston, George Foreman, and Joe Frazier are considered among the sport's most impressive accomplishments.

Jack Dempsey

Professional sports' first real superstar athlete, Jack Dempsey's power punching and ferocious style began the era of modern heavyweight boxing and elevated the sport to the level of major league baseball in popularity. Dempsey's influence can be seen in the fighting styles of Joe Frazier, Roberto Duran, and Mike Tyson, all of whom competed more than a half-century after Dempsey's retirement.

Joe Louis

Joe Louis, the legendary "Brown Bomber," held the heavyweight title for a record 12 years and made 25 successful title defenses, more than any boxing champion in any weight class. The second Black heavyweight champion (after Jack Johnson), Louis was a hero in the Black community of the 1930s and '40s, and his sensational first-round knockout of Germany's Max Schmeling during World War II afforded him similar status around the world.

Rocky Marciano

The only heavyweight champion to retire undefeated (49–0, 43 KOs), Rocky Marciano possessed knockout power in either hand and a seemingly granite jaw. The right cross with which he knocked out Jersey Joe Walcott to win the title in 1951 is considered one of the single greatest punches ever thrown.

Sugar Ray Leonard

The darling of the outstanding 1976 US Olympic team, Sugar Ray Leonard won titles in divisions ranging from welterweight (147) to super middleweight (168). His fights with Thomas Hearns and Roberto Duran were classics, but his greatest performance may have come against Marvelous Marvin Hagler, whom he defeated for the middleweight title in 1987 after not having fought for nearly three years. His soft-drink commercial with his young son was the first major endorsement deal awarded to a professional boxer.

Mike Tyson

The most famous, if not the best, fighter of the past 40 years, Mike Tyson's career was marked by ferocity in the ring and controversy outside it. Tyson became the youngest heavyweight champion (20 years, five months) in 1986, and at his peak, the world stopped to watch on the nights Tyson fought. But his glory days were short-lived: his 91-second KO of Michael Spinks, three days before Tyson's 22nd birthday, turned out to be the high point of his career.

Manny Pacquiao

The remarkable Filipino Manny Pacquiao began boxing in 1996 as a 106-pounder and went on to win world titles in eight divisions, from flyweight (112 pounds) to welterweight (147 pounds). He was also elected to the Senate in the Philippines and as of this writing (2025) continues to box professionally despite having been voted into the International Boxing Hall of Fame, an honor usually afforded only retired boxers, in 2025. Pacquiao's fights have generated a reported $1.2 billion.

Floyd Mayweather Jr.

The only boxing champion to match Marciano's record of retiring undefeated (49–0, plus a victory over Conor McGregor, an MMA fighter making his boxing debut), Floyd Mayweather Jr.'s nickname of "Money" was well-earned — his fights reportedly generated nearly $2 billion in revenue and, with endorsements, earned him approximately $1.2 billion. His 2015 showdown with Pacquiao, which Mayweather won by decision, was the most widely viewed boxing match in history, generating a reported 4.6 million pay-per-view purchases.

Christy Martin

There were women boxers before Christy Martin, but none as big as "The Coal Miner's Daughter," who became the first female boxer on the cover of *Sports Illustrated* and the first woman inducted into the International Boxing Hall of Fame. Promoted by Don King, she was featured on the undercards of many world title bouts, including those of Mike Tyson and Julio Cesar Chavez.

Claressa Shields

In addition to being the first American boxer to win back-to-back Olympic gold medals in 2012 and 2016 (and as of this writing, the most recent US boxer to win gold), Claressa Shields is the only female boxer ever to be recognized as a champion by all four boxing ratings organizations in three different weight classes. She is also one of just three women, along with Amanda Serrano and Naoko Fujioka, to win titles in five weight classes.

Honorable Mentions

- **Henry Armstrong:** The only boxer in history to hold world titles in three weight classes simultaneously (featherweight, lightweight, and welterweight), Armstrong was 27–0 in 1937 alone, scoring 26 knockouts.
- **Sam Langford:** A 5-foot-6 fireplug who fought for 24 years in every weight class from lightweight to heavyweight and was ducked by champions Jack Johnson and Jack Dempsey.

- **Archie Moore:** Known as "The Ol' Mongoose," the former light-heavyweight champion boxed for 28 years, had 220 bouts and scored 132 knockouts. His second-to-last fight, at age 48, was against a young heavyweight named Cassius Clay.
- **Willie Pep:** Former featherweight champion nicknamed "Will 'o the Wisp" because of his leatherproof defense, Pep had 240 fights and lost only 11.
- **Sandy Saddler:** The tall (5-foot-8½) rangy featherweight knocked out Willie Pep twice and was only stopped once — in his second professional fight! Went on to win 145 of 163 bouts.

Chapter 18

Ten Pivotal Fights

There have been countless thousands of professional and amateur boxing matches since the 18th century, and to whittle down that vast number of bouts to a list of "best" or "most important" boxing matches is as foolish as trying to step into the ring with Joe Louis or Muhammad Ali. However, it's possible to designate two handfuls of historic bouts as particularly significant. In my opinion, the following 10 fights were among the most impactful in the long history of man's oldest sport.

Sullivan–Corbett (1897)

The first heavyweight title fight fought with gloves. This bout also introduced "scientific" boxing in the form of "Gentleman Jim" Corbett, a slick jab-and-move fighter who easily outclassed the crude John L. Sullivan, knocking him out in the 21st round.

Johnson–Jeffries (1910)

The bout that started a century-long search for the Great White Hope. Former champion Jeffries was coaxed out of a five-year retirement to "rescue" the White race from Johnson, a proud and flamboyant man who was the first Black heavyweight champion. Johnson toyed with Jeffries before brutally KO-ing him in the

15th round, touching off race riots around the country and preventing a Black man from holding the title until Joe Louis came along two decades later.

Dempsey–Willard (1919)

The fight that propelled boxing to the forefront of spectator sports and made Dempsey a superstar on a par with Babe Ruth. Dempsey's three-round destruction of Jess Willard remains probably the most one-sided beating of a champion by a challenger and prompted a series of unprecedented million-dollar gates and crowds of over 100,000 to see Dempsey fight.

Tunney–Dempsey (1927)

Nearly a century later, it is still considered the most controversial fight in heavyweight history. Dempsey, who had lost his title to Gene Tunney the year before, was being soundly beaten again when he landed a pulverizing four-punch combination, dropping Tunney in the seventh round. But his refusal to abide by a new rule requiring a boxer scoring a knockdown to retreat to a neutral corner cost Dempsey at least five precious seconds, allowing Tunney to recover and go on to win a decision. Arguments still rage over whether the delay cost Dempsey the fight.

Louis–Schmeling II (1938)

In the most politically significant fight of the 20th century, Louis, having been knocked out by Schmeling two years previously and under tremendous pressure to defeat this symbol of Nazi Germany, scored an overwhelming first-round knockout before 80,000 fans in Yankee Stadium. Reportedly, Hitler shut off the German broadcast of the fight before the ending.

Liston–Clay (1964)

The fight that ushered in the age of Muhammad Ali, trash-talk, and mega-fights. The boxer then known as Cassius Clay taunted, outboxed, and humiliated Sonny Liston, at the time considered unbeatable and every bit as fearsome as Mike Tyson would be 20 years later. So complete was the beating that Liston quit on his stool after six rounds, claiming a shoulder injury.

Ali–Frazier trilogy (1971–1975)

The greatest boxing trilogy in any weight class saw Frazier winning the first match in 1971, Ali evening the score three years later, and stopping Frazier after 14 furious rounds in the Thrilla in Manila in 1975. But that doesn't begin to tell the story of a rivalry that divided the country along racial lines and spawned bitterness that remained between the two men until their deaths.

Tyson–Spinks (1988)

The antithesis of the Ali–Frazier series, the battle for the undisputed heavyweight title between Mike Tyson and Michael Spinks was highly anticipated but turned out to be anticlimactic. The 21-year-old Tyson, at his destructive peak, needed just 91 seconds to KO Spinks. It turned out to be the high point of his career.

Tyson–Douglas (1990)

In a fight that some consider the most shocking upset in boxing history, Tyson, a 42–1 favorite, was dismantled and knocked out by Buster Douglas, a talented career underachiever, in 10 rounds at the Tokyo Dome. With the loss, the cloak of invincibility that engulfed the young Tyson and intimidated so many of his opponents was permanently stripped away.

Mayweather–Pacquiao (2015)

The richest and most widely viewed boxing event in history turned out to be as big a dud as Tyson–Spinks, only longer. Floyd Mayweather Jr. and Manny Pacquiao, both past their prime and meeting arguably five years later than they should have, lumbered through 12 largely uneventful rounds to a Mayweather decision. Still, more than four million households shelled out up to $100 for the pay-per-view telecast, generating upward of $410 million in gross revenue, both records.

Chapter 19

Ten (or So) Great Boxing Books

Throughout history, boxing has been an attractive and fertile subject for great writers because of the sheer drama of the sport, the danger it involves, and the wide variety of characters who make up its colorful fabric. Ernest Hemingway, Norman Mailer, Joyce Carol Oates, and countless others have been fascinated by the sport and its participants, and have left behind a treasure trove of great boxing books, both fictional and factual. In no particular order, here's a partial list of some of my favorites.

The Sweet Science, A. J. Liebling

Boxing's most elegant stylist crafted these essays for *The New Yorker* in the '40s and '50s. They capture the magic of the likes of Joe Louis, Sugar Ray Robinson, and Rocky Marciano, among others, in a way no writer had before, or since.

The Professional, W. C. Heinz

A boxing novel that explores the complicated relationship between a sports writer and his subject and exposes both the glories and the heartbreak of the fight game. The ending is unforgettable.

The Arc of Boxing: The Rise and Decline of the Sweet Science, Mike Silver

A history of boxing with an irresistible twist: The author makes a strong case that boxers of the past were superior to the boxers of today, with evidence to back it up. A fascinating and informative read.

Ghosts of Manila: The Fateful Blood Feud between Muhammad Ali and Joe Frazier, Mark Kram

A chronicle of the stormy — and sometimes surprisingly friendly — relationship between Muhammad Ali and Joe Frazier, two men forever linked by their classic trilogy of fights, told from Frazier's viewpoint. Essential reading for anyone wanting to understand the dynamic between these two great warriors and how they were shaped by the tumultuous era they lived in.

The Harder They Fall, Budd Schulberg

Probably the best boxing novel ever written, it details the tragic story of Toro Molina, a giant who can't really fight but who, through a series of fixed matches, makes it to a world title shot that ends in a brutal beating and a devastating ending. Made into a classic 1957 movie with Humphrey Bogart and Rod Steiger.

Baddest Man: The Making of Mike Tyson, Mark Kriegel

The best book written on the influences that shaped Mike Tyson, from his childhood up to the crowning moment of his career, his 91-second knockout of Michael Spinks when Tyson was still only 21 years old. Volume one of a two-volume biography.

Sting Like a Bee: The Muhammad Ali Story, Jose Torres

The former light-heavyweight champion's intimate and revealing look at Muhammad Ali, from his amateur days up to the night he confronted Joe Frazier in the "Fight of the Century."

Unforgivable Blackness: The Rise and Fall of Jack Johnson, Geoffrey C. Ward

The story of the first Black heavyweight champion is a gut-wrenching look at a shameful period in American history: the mistreatment and ultimate exile of a great athlete due to the color of his skin.

In This Corner . . . !: 42 World Champions Tell Their Stories, Peter Heller

A fascinating oral history of boxing from the mouths of Sugar Ray Robinson, Willie Pep, Floyd Patterson, Rocky Graziano, and 38 other former world champions from boxing's golden age.

Sweet Thunder: The Life and Times of Sugar Ray Robinson, Wil Haygood

The definitive biography of boxing's greatest all-around performer explores what it was like to be the king of Black America in the Harlem of the 1940s.

The Legendary Champions, Rex Lardner

A coffee-table-sized book that documents the history of the heavyweight championship, from the bareknuckle days through the mega-fights of Jack Dempsey in the Roaring '20s. Great photographs to go along with lively and informative prose.

The Devil and Sonny Liston, Nick Tosches

From the first paragraph, you will be hooked on the tragic story of the most feared and fearsome of heavyweight champions, decades before Mike Tyson or George Foreman.

The Fight, Norman Mailer

Typically self-indulgent but still gripping account of the "Rumble in the Jungle," the unforgettable fight in which Muhammad Ali vanquished the seemingly invincible George Foreman in Zaire. The inspiration for the Oscar-winning documentary *When We Were Kings.*

Chapter 20

(Almost) Ten Great Boxing Movies

Movies about boxing tend to be cliché-ridden affairs with fight scenes that are so cartoonishly exaggerated they could not possibly happen in real life (see *Rocky, Rocky II, III,* and *IV*). But there are two handfuls of films that attempt to show the fight game in all its tawdry glory that I can recommend without reservation.

When We Were Kings (1996)

Oscar-winning documentary about the "Rumble in the Jungle," the dramatic 1974 heavyweight title bout in which Muhammad Ali dethroned George Foreman. A little too much Norman (Mailer) and not enough Foreman (George), but the behind-the-scenes footage is spectacular, as is the fight, which is shown in truncated form. Also, great music from James Brown, the Spinners, and B. B. King. A rousing, uplifting experience.

The Set-Up (1949)

A hard-as-nails film noir about an aging boxer, played by Robert Ryan, expected to deliberately lose his final fight so mobsters can cash a bet. His pride won't allow him to take the dive, however, and the consequences are severe. Gripping and brutal drama.

The Prizefighter and the Lady (1933)

This indispensable historical document stars Max Baer, on the verge of challenging Primo Carnera for the heavyweight title in real life, essentially playing himself as a happy-go-lucky playboy who can also deliver a knockout punch. Baer is pretty good in the role, even singing and dancing at one point, and the final scene of his title bout against Carnera (playing himself) is eerily close to what their actual fight looked like the following year.

Raging Bull (1980)

Not so much a boxing film as a character study of a man (Robert DeNiro playing Jake LaMotta) who is addicted to violence and how it causes both his rise and his fall. Exceptional performances by all, but the fight scenes are a little over the top.

Requiem for a Heavyweight (1962)

Another heartbreaker, this one about a washed-up heavyweight (played beautifully by Anthony Quinn) struggling to find his way in life after the end of his career. Written by Rod Serling, also starring Jackie Gleason as a sleazy manager and offering a glimpse of a young Muhammad Ali, then known as Cassius Clay, in the film's opening scene.

Fat City (1972)

A different kind of boxing film, this one doesn't deal with the glitz and glamor of championship boxing but with the down-and-dirty world of the club fighter, a journeyman performer with no hope of ever reaching the big time. Stacy Keach is outstanding as the main character and John Huston's direction captures the bleakness of the world he lives in.

Ali: The Fighter (1973)

An incredible but hard to find documentary about the epic 1971 heavyweight title fight between challenger Muhammad Ali and champion Joe Frazier at Madison Square Garden, at the time the most widely anticipated and watched sporting event in history. Great footage of both camps in the lead-up to the fight, and an added bonus for real boxing fans is that the fight itself is presented in its entirety with live crowd noise but no commentary, recreating the experience of being in the arena on that magical night.

Somebody Up There Likes Me (1956)

A surprisingly warts-and-all biography of Rocky Graziano, a New York City tough who overcame an early criminal record and a dishonorable discharge from the US Army to become the middleweight champion of the world. Paul Newman overdoes the dese-dem-dose in the title role but the script is hard-hitting and no white-wash of a flawed but ultimately likeable character.

Glossary

apron The two-foot area between the ropes and the outer edge of the ring, designed to keep a downed boxer from falling out of the ring onto the floor.

athletic commission A state agency responsible for the licensing of boxers, trainers, managers, and promoters; the enforcing of the rules of the ring; ensuring the fitness and safety of the boxers, the integrity of the bouts, and the payments to the parties involved.

bob and weave A style of defense in which the boxer relies on movement of the head and upper body to avoid punches, rather than blocking or catching them with the gloves. Used by Jack Dempsey, Joe Frazier, Roberto Duran, and Mike Tyson, among others.

body punch A blow that lands above the waistband of a boxer's trunks and below the head.

bucket carrier Generally the third person in a boxer's corner, whose chief responsibility is to gather and carry the supplies needed during the fight (ice, water, cotton swabs, etc.) and provide them to the trainer or cut person as necessary.

butt Striking an opponent with the head. Butts often happen accidentally in the ring, but an intentional butt is a foul that can result in disqualification.

canvas The floor surface of a boxing ring, which is stretched tight over a firm, one-inch-thick foam rubber pad.

catch A defensive move in which a boxer stops an opponent's punch with their open glove.

chief second The person in a boxer's corner responsible for giving advice to the boxer between rounds. The chief second is usually the boxer's trainer.

clean punching Refers to legal blows that can be clearly seen by the judges to have landed effectively. One of the four standards used by judges to score a fight, along with effective aggression, ring generalship, and defense.

clinch (or tie up) A defensive move in which a boxer immobilizes an opponent's arms either by grabbing them or locking down the opponent's gloves under their armpits.

combination A series of two or more punches.

conventional or orthodox boxer One who stands with the left foot forward and jabs with the left hand. Usually a right-handed boxer.

corner pads The narrow, vertical foam pads in each corner that protect the boxers from making contact with the steel turnbuckles that support the ropes.

corner person Any of the (usually) three people working in a boxer's corner between rounds.

counterpunch A punch that is thrown in response to an opponent's punch, often used to take advantage of the opening created by a missed punch.

cover up A defensive move in which a boxer brings both gloves up in front of the face while tucking the chin down into the chest, creating a protective clamshell against an opponent's flurry.

cross A power punch thrown with the rear hand, delivered straight from the shoulder and with full weight transfer due to hip rotation and foot pivot, usually following a jab.

cut person A member of the boxer's corner whose chief responsibility is the closing of cuts and controlling of bleeding between rounds.

decision The conclusion of a fight in which a boxer is determined the winner by virtue of the judges awarding them more points than the opponent.

defense The art of evading punches, either by movement of the head or body or blocking with the gloves.

disqualification When a boxer is declared the loser of a bout by the referee due to repeated or flagrant fouls. The most famous disqualification in boxing history occurred when Mike Tyson bit off a chunk of Evander Holyfield's ear in the third round of a 1997 heavyweight title bout.

draw A decision in which neither fighter is declared the winner due either to all three judges scoring the bout even or to two judges scoring different fighters the winner and the third judge scoring the bout even.

effective aggression Pressure applied by a boxer that results in the landing of clean and damaging blows. One of the four standards used by judges for scoring a fight, along with clean punching, ring generalship, and defense.

feint A fake or threatened punch, or any move designed to trick your opponent into providing an opening or thinking you're about to throw one hand when in fact you're throwing the other.

foul Any illegal action in the ring, including low blows, rabbit punches, intentional butts, hitting an opponent who is down, hitting on the break of a clinch, or hitting after the bell. Serious and repeated fouls can result in disqualification.

hook A power punch thrown usually with the front hand in which the arm is in an L-shaped position, the torso turns sharply, and the fist impacts the side of the head or body.

jab A straight punch thrown with the front hand, generally used to keep an opponent at a distance or to set up other punches.

judge One of three individuals at ringside whose responsibility is to score the fight on the 10-point must system. Judges are instructed to use four standard yardsticks in assessing the winner of a round: clean punching, defense, effective aggression, and ring generalship.

knockdown timekeeper The person responsible for beginning the count when a boxer is knocked down. The referee picks up the timekeeper's count in progress after directing the fighter scoring the knockdown to a neutral corner and continues counting until the downed boxer rises or is counted out.

knockout The most definitive conclusion of a fight, when one fighter is knocked down by a legal blow and cannot rise within the referee's count of 10, which, incidentally, may not precisely correspond to a count of 10 seconds.

live gate The amount of money taken in from ticket sales to a boxing match. In the pre-television era, the live gate was the main source of revenue for paying the boxers.

low blow A foul blow that lands below the waistband of an opponent's trunks. Excessive low blows can result in points deductions, and in extreme cases, disqualification.

main event The headline bout of a boxing card, usually the last or second to last bout of the night, generally matching two high-profile boxers in a significant bout.

majority decision A decision in which two judges score one fighter the winner and the third scores the bout even.

majority draw A decision in which two of the three judges score the bout even, resulting in a draw.

manager A boxer's representative who negotiates with the promoter on behalf of the boxer. The manager's payment ranges from 10% to 33% of a fighter's purse. It is an illegal conflict of interest for a promoter to also be a manager or for a manager to work for a promoter.

mandatory 8-count The referee's count of eight over a knocked-down fighter, after which he determines whether the fighter is able to continue in the bout.

matchmaker An employee of the promoter whose job it is to find boxers for the undercard and then match them according to experience, skill level, and fighting style with the aim of creating a competitive and entertaining fight card.

neutral corner Either of the two corners that are not assigned to a boxer.

no contest A fight in which neither boxer is declared the winner or loser, often due to an accidental foul resulting in a stoppage occurring too early in the bout for the scorecards to be used. In a 12-round championship fight, four rounds must be completed before a winner can be declared.

parry A defensive move in which a boxer uses the outside of the glove to knock an opponent's punch away, much like the motion of shooing away a swarm of gnats, or uses the inside of the glove to knock a punch down.

promoter The person or organization responsible for staging a boxing program, securing financing, arranging for a site, and negotiating purses for the fighters.

purse The negotiated amount a boxer will be paid for a particular fight. Purses can be flat fees, percentages of live gate and broadcast revenues, or a combination of the two.

rabbit punch A foul blow delivered to the back or side of an opponent's neck.

referee The third person in the ring, responsible for enforcing the rules, penalizing fighters who commit fouls, breaking clinches, and stopping the fight if determined that one fighter cannot continue.

ring The square, rope-enclosed area in which a boxing match is contested. There is no standard size for a boxing ring; they range from 16 to 24 feet per side and are elevated approximately four feet off the floor.

ring generalship The ability of a boxer to control the tempo and style of a fight as well as where in the ring it is fought — in the center of the ring, along its perimeter, or on the ropes. One of the four standards by which boxing matches are judged, along with clean punching, defense, and effective aggression.

ringpost Any of the four poles that stand in a corner of the ring supporting the ropes.

roll A defensive move in which a boxer ducks under an opponent's punch and moves the upper body in a circular motion to position themself to land a counterpunch.

ropes The barriers that delineate the outer edges of a boxing ring. There are four ropes enclosing a boxing ring, the lowest one set 13 inches above the canvas and the highest at 52 inches, separated at 13-inch intervals.

sanctioning fee The amount of money charged by a sanctioning organization in exchange for its blessing on a title fight. Sanctioning fees can run into the hundreds of thousands of dollars.

sanctioning organization An autonomous body that awards titles and ranks boxers. Currently, there are four major boxing sanctioning organizations: the World Boxing Council (WBC), the World Boxing Association (WBA), the International Boxing Federation (IBF), and the World Boxing Organization (WBO). Each recognizes its own champions and often ranks different boxers in each weight class than the others.

second Another way to refer to a boxer's corner person.

shoeshine A flurry of fast punches to the body resembling the motion of shining shoes with a cloth.

site fee The amount a venue agrees to pay a promoter in exchange for hosting a boxing event. The site generally keeps the proceeds from ticket sales and concessions.

slip A defensive move in which a boxer moves the head slightly to one side to avoid a punch.

southpaw A left-handed boxer, or one who stands with the right foot forward and jabs with the right hand.

split decision A decision in which two of the three judges determine the same fighter to be the winner, and the third judge scores the fight in favor of the opponent.

technical draw When a fight is stopped prematurely due to an accidental foul (usually a headbutt) and the scores are even at the time of the stoppage.

technical knockout The conclusion of a fight in which the referee, the ringside physician, or the fighter's corner determine a fighter cannot continue due to an injury caused by legal blows or the taking of too many punches. Also known as a stoppage.

technical win When a fight is stopped early due to an accidental cut or headbutt, and the fight has gone past a certain number of rounds (usually four), the bout goes to the scorecards for a decision.

10-point must system The universal method of scoring professional boxing matches in which the boxer determined to have won a round receives 10 points and the opponent nine or fewer, depending on how one-sided the round was. Boxers scoring a knockdown are generally awarded 10-8 rounds, or even 10-7 if multiple knockdowns are scored. Rarely if ever are 10-6 rounds scored.

timekeeper The person responsible for timing the rounds and rest periods and ringing the bell to begin and end each round.

trainer The person who directs the boxer's workout routine, helps determine strategy, and delivers advice in the corner between rounds of a fight. The trainer is generally the chief second in a boxer's corner.

unanimous decision A decision in which all three judges have determined the same boxer to be the winner.

undercard The bouts preceding and leading up to the main event. The bout immediately preceding the main event is known as the **semi-final** and is often a title fight or similarly significant bout matching two highly regarded boxers.

uppercut A power punch that comes up from the floor with the boxer's palm facing upward, usually intended to land under an opponent's chin.

Index

C

D

G

H

I

J

K

L

M

N

O

P

T

U

V

W

Y

About the Author

Wallace Matthews started out in 1977 as a Golden Gloves boxer, became a boxing writer and columnist in the early 1980s, and now works as a boxing instructor and personal fitness trainer. He covered all the major fights of Mike Tyson, Evander Holyfield, Sugar Ray Leonard, Marvelous Marvin Hagler, Thomas Hearns, Oscar de la Hoya, Manny Pacquiao, and Floyd Mayweather Jr. during boxing's last Golden Age of 1985–2005 for publications such as *New York Newsday*, *The New York Times*, *New York Post*, and *New York Daily News*, and served as a television boxing analyst for ESPN, Showtime, NBC, and CBS. He was inducted into the International Boxing Hall of Fame in Canastota, New York, in 2024 in the Observer category. He lives on Long Island.

Acknowledgments

Although I only began writing *Boxing For Dummies* in the fall of 2025, this book has been in the works for more than 60 years, ever since the day my dad brought home two pairs of boxing gloves for my brother and me, since we were always fighting anyway. That started a lifelong love affair and, eventually, a professional association with the sport of boxing that continues to this day.

Along the way, I owe a tremendous debt of gratitude to many individuals, starting with my late dad, Wallace, to whom this book is dedicated; my beautiful and patient wife, Leslie; and my wonderful children, Steven and Cassandra.

When I began writing about boxing professionally in 1984, I was helped tremendously along the way by such gifted professional journalists as Budd Schulberg, Barney Nagler, Bob Waters, Jim Murray, Michael Katz, Ed Schuyler, Pat Putnam, and Bert Randolph Sugar, and was fortunate to work alongside gifted younger writers such as Mark Kriegel, Jon Saraceno, Dave Raffo, Phil Berger, and countless others who became not just colleagues, but friends. And a huge thank you to the late Dick Sandler, my first editor at *Newsday*, who had the foresight — or insanity — to take a chance on a kid out of his high school sports bullpen and hand him the boxing beat.

The advice and education I received from the great boxing trainers of the '40s, '50s, and '60s — men such as Eddie Futch, Ray Arcel, Emanuel Steward, Gil Clancy, Angelo Dundee, Richie Giachetti, Al Gavin, and Don Turner — could not be bought at any price. They were unfailingly generous with their time and knowledge.

I am indebted to the wonderful people who populate my five-times-a-week boxing class at the Huntington YMCA. Their dedication to learning the intricacies of this most difficult sport and the herculean effort they give at every session is truly humbling and makes me enjoy this job more than any I've ever had.

Most of all, thanks to the boxers themselves, who are the most cooperative and candid athletes I ever had the privilege to cover. They give more to the sport of boxing and its fans than either could ever hope to give back.

Dedication

To my late dad, also named Wallace Matthews, who loved Floyd Patterson and instilled in me a lifelong passion for this oldest and greatest of sports.

Publisher's Acknowledgments

Acquisitions Editor: Jennifer Yee
Project Editor: Christopher Morris
Copy Editor: Amy Handy
Managing Editor: Murari Mukundan
Production Editor: Umeshkumar Rajasekhar
Cover Image: Mike Harrington/Getty Images